Following Historic Trails

Famous Indian Leaders

Philomena Hauck

and

Kathleen M. Snow

Detselig Enterprises Ltd.
Calgary, Alberta

Following Historic Trails

Famous Indian Leaders

Canadian Cataloguing in Publication Data

Hauck, Philomena, 1927 -
  Famous Indian leaders

  (following historic trails)
  Bibliography: p.
  ISBN 0-920490-99-9

  1. Indians of North America – Biography – Juvenile
literature. 2. Indians of North America – Canada –
Biography – Juvenile literature. I. Snow, Kathleen
Mary, 1918- II. Title. III. Series.
E89.H38 1989   j970.004'97   C89-091204-1

©1989 by Detselig Enterprises Limited
P.O. Box G 399
Calgary, Alberta T3A 2G3

Printed in Canada   SAN 115-0324   ISBN 0-920490-99-9

About the Authors

Kathleen Snow received her B.A. in English from the University of Alberta, her B.L.S. from the University of Washington, and her B.Ed. and M.A.(English) from the University of Calgary. She has worked with the Calgary Public Library, the Calgary Board of Education, and she was an Associate Professor in the Faculty of Education at the University of Calgary. Kathleen Snow is a member of the Canadian and Alberta Library Associations.

Philomena Hauck was born in Ireland and came to Canada in 1955 as a high school English teacher. She later became a school librarian and then Associate Professor and Director of the Education Materials Centre, University of Calgary. Philomena Hauck has a B.A., B. Comm., M. Ed. and Ph.D. and she is a member of the Canadian Library Association and the International Association of School Librarians.

Detselig Enterprises Ltd. appreciates the financial
assistance for its 1989 publishing program from

Alberta Foundation for the Literary Arts
Canada Council
Department of Communications
Alberta Culture

Contents

Introduction

When Samuel de Champlain made his first voyage to Canada, the country was inhabited by over 200 000 native people. As far as we can tell, these people had left their homelands in eastern Asia many centuries before and made their way across the Bering Strait to North America in several migrations. In time, they scattered over the entire continent from Alaska to Tierra del Fuego in South America, bringing their skills and customs with them and developing new ones. Different groups developed in different ways and new languages evolved.

By Champlain's time, there were over 50 tribes in Canada. These tribes fall into seven broad categories: (a) the tribes of the eastern woodlands, or the Algonkians, (b) the Iroquoians, (c) the prairie tribes, (d) the Indians of the west coast, (e) the Indians of the British Columbia interior and (f) the Indians of the Northwest Territories (g) and the Inuit. Some of the tribes had hunting grounds both north and south of the present Canada-United States border. The Iroquois nations, for example, spilled over from present-day New York into southern Ontario, and the Blackfoot hunted the buffalo on the Canadian and the American prairies.

The Indian way of life depended largely on climate and available foodstuffs. The abundant supply of food and the mild climate made life easy for the west coast people, such as the Nootka. Instead of roaming in search of food, they lived in semi-permanent villages and enjoyed elaborate feasts, known as potlatches. In their leisure time, they became adept at carving and painting. The Indians of the Northwest Territories were far too busy keeping themselves alive to devote much time to amusement or art. Constantly on the move in small bands in search of game, they had no real tribal unity. On the other hand, the Iroquois who lived in fertile lands with a more temperate climate, farmed the land and developed an elaborate system of government.

The early French settlers first came in

contact with the Algonkians, a group composed of several tribes all speaking the same language or dialect. Their hunting grounds, extending all the way from Newfoundland to the Great Lakes, were made up of dense forests and scrubland dotted with rugged rocks and boulders. In the few fertile patches such as inland Nova Scotia, people like the Mic Mac grew maize and beans, but for the most part the people lived by hunting and fishing.

In late fall, the Algonkians set out in small groups in search of moose, bear, beaver and other animals. Summer was the time for fishing, although they also caught fish in winter through holes dug in the ice. Because they were always on the move, they had few possessions. Even their dwellings made of birch bark rolls or skins attached to poles were portable. In winter, they travelled on snowshoes, often dragging a toboggan behind them, and in summer, they skimmed the waters in their graceful canoes.

Although the Algonkians were more numerous than the Iroquoians to the south, they lived in fear of their powerful neighbors. On his arrival in Quebec, Champlain became friendly with the Algonkians and they asked him to join them in attacking their old foes. Champlain agreed. In 1609, he launched a successful attack, and the following year, he repeated the victory. From that time on, the Iroquois were enemies of the French.

At the time, Champlain thought he had done the right thing. Had he refused to help the Algonkians, they would probably have turned against him and driven him and his handful of followers out of the country. In the long run, however, his decision would cause the French a lot of grief.

Unlike the wandering Algonkians, the Iroquois lived in semi-permanent villages. The Iroquois league, sometimes called the Five Nations consisted of the Mohawks, the Oneidas, the Onondagas, the Cayugas and the Senecas, to which were added the Tuscaroras in 1722. The Hurons came from the same stock as the Iroquois and spoke the same language, but the two groups split apart.

The Iroquois were far more advanced than all the other nations. They had a well developed system of laws with a Grand Council to settle major common concerns, although each nation was allowed to run its own affairs. Leaders (or sachems) selected by the noble women of the nation were fine statesmen and great speakers. As warriors, the Iroquois had no match. Contrary to some accounts, they did not make war for its own sake. When they went on the warpath, it was to protect or extend their hunting grounds – and to bring about a lasting peace. Strange as it may seem, they fought hard to put an end to war! Nations were first invited to join in the Great Peace, and if encouragement did not work, the Iroquois used force.

Like the other Indian nations, the Iroquois had no such thing as a standing army. Although bravery was highly prized, a man could join a war party or leave it when he wished. As a result, wars were not prolonged affairs with one large army facing another. They were short, swift attacks and clever ambushes. People who lived by hunting and fishing could not undertake a large campaign, so they used every trick they knew to defeat their enemies. Accustomed to military discipline, the Europeans accused the native people of unfair fighting. The natives were also accused of cruelty. However, the Europeans with their racks and torture chambers were cruel in a different way. With some grisly exceptions, the torture of prisoners was not common among the native people. Captives were usually adopted into the tribe, and there are several stories of prisoners who preferred to stay with the Indians rather than returning to their own homes.

After the Hurons split away from the Iroquois league, the two groups were constantly at one another's throats. The Hurons lived in Ontario, between Lake Simcoe and Georgian Bay. Like the other Iroquoians, they were farmers and lived in semi-permanent villages. They also did some hunting and fishing and they were shrewd traders. The Hurons bartered maize, tobacco and fish nets, in exchange for dried meat, furs and canoes. Trade was chiefly with the Algonkians. With the arrival of the French came a great demand for beaver pelts, and the Hurons acted as middlemen between the French and the Algonkians. They exchanged axes, kettles and other French goods for the beavers they obtained from their northern neighbors.

As a token of their friendship with the white man, the Hurons agreed to accept Jesuit missionaries. In time, they grew to respect the priests for their bravery and kindness, and several Christian missions were set up in Huronia. With the white man came the white man's diseases – measles, smallpox and tuberculosis. Having no immunity to the new diseases, the unfortunate Hurons dropped like flies and in a few short years the Huron population was cut in half.

Meanwhile, their Iroquois neighbors to the south were trading with the Dutch and New Englanders. The more they became accustomed to European goods, the better they liked them. To get the new utensils, they had to have lots of fur, but beavers were scarce in Iroquois country. Obviously the Iroquois had to extend their hunting grounds.

In 1642, the Iroquois began to receive arms from the Dutch. With their new and powerful weapons, they unleashed an attack on the Huron people. In the ensuing struggle, the Huron nation, already weakened from disease, was destroyed. Driven from their homes and deprived of food, the Hurons scattered in all directions and their trading monopoly with the French came to an end. The destruction of Huronia brought the Iroquois less than they had hoped. In a few years, Algonkian tribes, particularly the Ottawa, took control of the western fur-trade.

The wars that plagued North America for the next 50 years were mainly caused by fur-trading rivalries. To make matters worse, the English and the French were often at war in Europe, and these conflicts spilled over into the New World. Drawn into the struggle between the two powers, the native people lost many of their young men. European diseases and alcohol took a terrible toll as well. As they became more dependent on the white man's tools and weapons, the native people also lost their old skills.

As long as the two European powers vied in North America, the Indians were courted by both sides. After the defeat of the French in 1763, the plight of the native people worsened. The eastern tribes were at the mercy of the English, who treated them more harshly than the French had ever done. Pontiac, the Ottawa war chief, fought to gain some independence for his people. He did not seek isolation, for the Indians could not live without European goods. He wanted his people to remain as a sovereign nation attached to the French.

After his defeat, the dream of a united Indian league faded. Toward the end of the American War of Independence, Joseph Brant tried in vain to bring the Indian people together to negotiate a better settlement for his people. With the remnants of his followers, Brant came to Canada and settled in southern Ontario. Gradually, the Canadian Indians east of the Great Lakes were assimilated with the white people or settled on reserves.

The native people on the vast prairies and in British Columbia were long untroubled by white settlers. The first account of the west coast Indians comes from the journals of Captain James Cook who visited the Nootka in 1778. Like the other west coast tribes, the Nootka lived in rows of large wooden houses which faced the ocean. Much of their food came from the sea and they had many different ways of catching fish. Although they knew nothing about farming, they did grow some tobacco. Unlike other native people, the west coast tribes did not smoke the tobacco, but ground it up and chewed it.

Their society was composed of three different ranks – nobles, commoners and slaves. Normally, titles were passed on from father to son or nephew. Slaves were generally prisoners-of-war and were treated well, but had no rights. The chiefs owned large houses and liked to outdo each other in splendor and prestige. Above all else, they set great store on gift giving. At a great feast, or potlatch, a chief would distribute slaves, canoes, furs, and sea-shells (which were used as currency) to the assembled guests. These favors were returned at later feasts.

The white strangers were well received on the west coast. The native people traded fish and furs for European axes, knives and metal of all kinds. As time went on, the people began to adopt the white man's customs and grew discontent with their old ways. The survivors were frequently scorned and called "siwashes," or savages. Today there are fewer than 15 000 natives left on the BC coast.

On the wide open prairies, vaguely known as "the wild west," there lived a number of Indian tribes, who depended on the buffalo for food, clothing and shelter. One of the earliest travellers to visit the prairies was Anthony Henday in 1754, but the white man did not settle on the land until 100 years later.

The strongest and most aggressive group among the prairie tribes was the Blackfoot nation, a loose alliance of three smaller nations – the Blood, the Piegan and the Blackfoot. Some people say the Blackfoot got the name from their black moccasins. Others claim that they were given the name because their feet were always black from the ashes of prairie fires.

All the prairie tribes lived in much the same way. Countless buffalo roamed the vast treeless land and the people spent most of their time hunting the animals. Buffalo flesh was their staple food. It could be eaten fresh or dried or made into pemmican – a dish made of finely ground dry buffalo meat, mixed with fat and crushed berries.

Before the horse was introduced, hunters tracked buffalo on foot, their possessions on a travois hauled by dogs. To cross rivers, people used "bull boats" made of buffalo hide inserted in a saucer-like frame made of saplings. Their cone-shaped teepees were made of buffalo skin attached to long poles. Inside the teepee, there was often an inner lining, also of skin, to keep out the cold. Clothes were made of fine skin for summer, and in winter, people wore heavier skins with the hair left on.

The coming of the white settlers brought trouble and confusion to the native people on the prairies. With the introduction of horses and firearms, they could kill many more buffalo. Buffalo hunters and adventurers arrived with their whiskey and their diseases, and tribe fought tribe for a share of the rich spoils. By 1879, the buffalo had virtually disappeared and the Indians were destitute.

To clear the way for white settlers, the Canadian government set aside Indian reserves and tried to turn buffalo hunters into instant farmers. Unable to adapt to the new ways, the people sank into apathy and despair. In time, many of the Blackfoot settled down to grow wheat and raise cattle, but other prairie tribes did not adjust so well.

Today there are over 450 000 native people in Canada. In recent years, they have been trying to forge a life for themselves which includes some of their old customs and the benefits of modern technology. A people with great pride and endurance, they hope to be allowed to participate in our society in dignity and peace.

Chapter One

Dekanahwideh

On the Mohawk Reserve at Desoronto, Ontario there stands a monument to Dekanahwideh, or the "Heavenly Messenger." According to Indian lore, he and the famous hero Hiawatha brought all the Iroquois tribes together into one great league, known to us as the Five Nations Confederacy. The league was well-organized and the members worked together a long time.

Centuries before the arrival of the white man, these people were one. They belonged to the Huron-Iroquois stock and they spoke the same language. In time, they split up into different tribes and spoke in different dialects, but they could all understand one another. Most of them lived in the beautiful rolling countryside south of Lake Ontario, in the present state of New York. From east to west the five Iroquois tribes were the Mohawks, the Oneidas, the Onondagas, the Cayugas and the Senecas. At a later date, another tribe, the Tuscaroras, was added. For many years, they fought among one another and with other tribes. What they needed was a leader to unite them and they found one in Dekanahwideh.

Accounts of Dekanahwideh's life are a strange blend of fact and fable. As one story goes, he was born in a Huron village in eastern Ontario some time in the fifteenth century. Before his birth, his mother dreamed that he would go to a far off country and bring peace to all the Iroquois nations. When he was a young boy, she told him about the dream and taught him to love his fellow people. Young Dekanahwideh grew up to be a strong and handsome man, honest and truthful in all his dealings, but his own tribe held him in low respect because he preferred peace to war. Besides, he had such a bad speech impediment that he could hardly talk.

When the time came for him to go on his mission of peace, he bade farewell to his mother saying:

I am ready now to go away from here. I will tell you that there is a tree on the top of a hill and you will have that for a sign whenever you wish to find out whether I am living or dead. You will take an axe and chop the tree and if the tree flows blood from the cut, you will know that I am beheaded and killed, but if you find no blood running from the tree, then you may know that my mission is successful.

That hill, near present-day Brantford, Ontario is still honored as a holy place by the Iroquois people.

As the legend continues, Dekanahwideh stepped into a beautiful white boat made of stone and glided across Lake Ontario to the home of the Onondagas. In that nation, there was an evil cannibal who lived alone and if he saw any man approach him, he would terrorize and kill him. As Dekanahwideh drew near the cannibal's abode, he saw the man carrying a human body into his hut. Shortly after, the man went to the nearby river to draw some water.

Dekanahwideh drew closer to the hut, climbed on the roof and peered through the smoke hole. Meanwhile, the cannibal returned, put a kettle over the fire and began to cook his meal. When it was cooked, he looked into the kettle and saw the reflection of Dekanahwideh's face in the water. The image of the kind and gentle face touched the wicked man's heart. There and then, he threw out the contents of the kettle and began to repent of his evil ways. Dekanahwideh descended from the roof and told the man about the message of peace and love. Thoughts of evil gone from his heart, the one-time cannibal agreed to return to his village and carry the message to his people.

About the same time, an Onondaga chieftain named Hiawatha had also grown weary of the bitter strife among his people. In his own tribe he did his best to form a peace council, but he was thwarted by a cruel chieftain named Atotarho. Atotarho was so crafty that people thought he was a wizard. In the story, he is pictured as a beast with snakes, instead of hair, on his head.

Hiawatha departed from the Onondaga country to carry his message to other tribes. Everywhere he went, he was well received, but the people could not forget their old hatreds. In the course of his wanderings, he met Dekanahwideh and the two men agreed to join forces. They made a good team. Hiawatha was a great orator, but his plans for peace were only vaguely thought out. Dekanahwideh spoke poorly, but he had definite ideas about how to bring the five nations together.

For a time the two men parted.

Hiawatha travelled from village to village spreading his friend's message and Dekanahwideh set out for the Mohawk nation.

The warlike Mohawks liked what they heard, but they were cautious. Before committing themselves to the new league, they wanted a sign from the Master of Life. To satisfy them, Dekanahwideh performed another wonder. Climbing a great tree overlooking the Mohawk River, he asked that the tree be cut down and thrown with him into the rapids. If he survived, they would agree to follow him.

The next morning the Mohawks saw a puff of smoke near the root of the tree. Seated by a fire calmly eating his breakfast was the "Heavenly Messenger." The Mohawks were convinced. Guided by Dekanahwideh, they agreed to establish the League of Peace. To this day, the Mohawks are considered to be the older brothers in the Five Nations Confederacy.

Joined by Hiawatha and the Mohawk leaders, Dekanahwideh proceeded west to the great village of the Oneidas. After hearing the message, the Oneidas called several council meetings and debated the subject for a long time. Finally, they decided to ratify a peace treaty with the Mohawk and to join them in extending the league. From there, Dekanahwideh and his allies proceeded to Cayuga country. The most peaceful of all the Five Nations, the Cayugas were readily convinced.

Their neighbors to the west, the Senecas, were divided at frist. Like the Mohawks, one group wanted Dekanahwideh to prove that he was indeed a heavenly messenger. Suddenly a great darkness shut out the sun and they were convinced. (An eclipse of the sun actually did take place in Seneca country in 1451.)

The Onondagas, led by the evil Atotarho, still held out. Led by Dekanahwideh and Hiawatha, the chiefs approached Atotarho's village chanting songs of peace. Then they made Atotarho a tempting proposal. He would be the leading chief in the new league and his village would be the capital of the federation, the site of the great council fire and the place where all the records were kept. Atotarho and his chiefs would have the right to summon the great council meetings and his tribe would have 14 members in the league, though no other nation would have more than ten.

Atotarho was won over. As the legend goes, Hiawatha (or, "He Who Combs") combed the serpents from Atotarho's hair and the former monster became human. The Five Nations Confederacy, or the "Great Peace" as the Iroquois called it, was taking shape.

To mark the solemn occasion, Dekanahwideh planted a white pine tree which was to be known as the Great Tree of Peace. Under the shade of the Great Tree would be spread the soft feathery down of the globe thistle for Atotarho and his chiefs to sit upon while they were holding their meetings. The tree would have four roots to show that the Great Peace would spread in all directions, and any nation that wished could come under its shade. On top of the tree would be the image of an eagle to symbolize the need to be always watchful. Into a great hole beside the tree, Dekanahwideh flung the weapons of war to show that the nations and all the people should remain at peace with one another.

According to Iroquois tradition, Dekanahwideh and Hiawatha then presented the new code of law which is followed to this day. The code was based on the ideal of universal peace and brotherhood. Disputes were to be settled in a democratic way and the rights of the individual were protected. Each of the five nations was allowed to settle internal disputes and follow its own customs, but the leaders worked together for the good of the whole federation.

The Great Council of all the nations was composed of 50 chiefs who held a meeting in Onondaga every five years and whenever an emergency arose. To avoid warlike pressure, the chiefs were to be sachems, not war chiefs. When a chief died or was unable to perform his duties, his successor would be elected from within his family. The deciding voice in the election rested with the chief woman (or "otiianer") of the family, such as the mother or the grandmother of the dead chief.

At his election, the new chief took the name of his predecessor, so that we can trace back a noble family for generations. The only exception is the name Dekanahwideh. Although the great man was a member of the first council, he forbade his people to appoint any successor to himself. "Let the others have successors," he said, "for others can advise you like them. But I am the founder of your League and no one else can do what I have done."

The Great Council was like a parliament. Everything was first debated in tribal groups and later in large session until agreement was reached. The business of the league was conducted in a very orderly fashion. Atotarho was the moderator and no one was allowed to interrupt a speaker. Later on, when Europeans had to deal with the Iroquois in making treaties, the white men were amazed at the dignity and power of the native speakers and the cleverness of their arguments.

Dekanahwideh introduced some important new laws. One of these related to blood feuds. In the past, if a member of one tribe killed a person from another, war was the inevitable result. The new law put a stop to this practice which had caused so much bloodshed. The dispute would be settled in council and the dead man's family would receive a gift to console them in their grief. There, the matter would be put to rest. The new law held the Iroquois together for many years, making them far more powerful than the Huron or the Algonqians.

Another law "to strengthen the house" related to funerals. Like other native tribes, the Iroquois had elaborate mourning rites. When a person died, it was the custom for the family to stop working, and weep and wail for days and weeks on end. Kettles, furs, and other treasures were thrown into the graves so that families were left destitute. Dekanahwideh and Hiawatha laid down a new rule. When a person died there would be a simple ceremony. Later, a small group would visit the relatives and present them with a gift of mourning wampum. The leader made a short speech telling the mourners "to cheer their minds, rekindle their hearth fires in peace and put their houses in order." This wise rule put an end to lavish ceremonies that were so wasteful of time and wealth.

Dekanahwideh believed that his League of Peace would extend all over the continent.

Other tribes were to be encouraged to join and Hiawatha was to be the messenger. The Iroquois name for the League was "Kanonsionni" or "The People of the Longhouse." This was their way of comparing the confederacy to a house, which could always be extended at each end, and within which everyone was like one great family.

When his work was done, Dekanahwideh called the Great Council together. At the meeting he urged the chiefs to preserve the peace and extend it throughout the land. He then embarked in a white canoe and paddled to the west.

After the American Revolution, the Mohawk chief, Joseph Brant, led many of the Iroquois north of the border into Canada. At their new home in the valley of the Grand River in Ontario, the refugees re-established the ancient league with all its laws and customs. The record keepers, the Onondagas, brought with them most of the old wampum belts which had been used to keep track of council decisions and treaties. To this day, the Iroquois on the Six Nations Reserve near Brantford, Ontario still visit the place where Dekanahwideh said farewell to his mother.

Over the years Dekanahwideh has been elevated to a kind of god. Nevertheless, his real achievements were important and long lasting. The league that he founded was the first example of a stable government on this continent.

Chapter Two

Chief Membertou

Long before European explorers came to Acadia, the land was peopled by roving bands of Indians, whom the French later called the Mic Macs. With their dark eyes, flowing black hair, and lean bodies smeared with animal grease to prevent mosquito bites, they were a sturdy and handsome race. In summer, the men wore loin cloths and loose cloaks tied near the shoulder with leather thongs, while the women wore similar cloaks held together with wide belts. In winter, both sexes wore large beaver coats tied at the back. They were hospitable people who were liberal with gifts of food and furs.

In 1605, when Champlain, Poutrincourt and their companions came to found the settlement of Port Royal, in present-day Annapolis Basin, they became friendly with the local Mic Macs and their great chief Membertou. By his own account, Membertou was over 100-years-old at the time and was already a married man when he met explorer Jacques Cartier in 1534. Since the Indian people had a different method of reckoning time than the Europeans, we cannot be sure of his exact age. We do know, however, that members of his tribe considered him an exceptional man, far excelling all others in wisdom, strength, and valor.

In appearance and habits, Membertou differed from other men of his tribe. He was a very tall man, bearded like a Frenchman, although scarcely any of the other Indians had hair on their faces. Unlike other chieftains, he never had more than one living wife. One chief, for example, had seven wives whom he paraded proudly before the horrified Jesuit priest, Father Biard. Father Biard knew that the influence of a chief was greatly strengthened by the alliances that many wives could bring. However, he was pleased that the great Membertou managed to preserve his authority without such alliances.

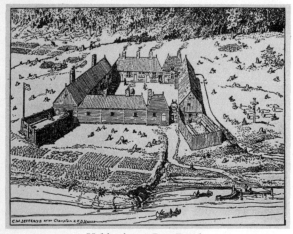

Habitation at Port Royal.
Etching by C.W. Jefferys.

In other ways too, Membertou was a unique man. As well as being the Sagamo (chief) of his tribe, he was also a sorcerer and a medicine man. A sorcerer was like a prophet. It was believed that he could foretell the weather, predict the place where good game could be found, and foresee the success of war parties. When the Mic Macs were hungry, they would visit Membertou and be told to go to a certain place for game. If they found the game, they were grateful for their Sagamo's powers; if they didn't, the explanation was that the beast had wandered away! As a medicine man, one of his powers was to drive out the evil spirit believed to cause illness. According to accounts, the medicine man went through a strange and complicated ritual, such as blowing on the afflicted part, chanting songs and spells, and casting out the Devil who tormented the patient. More helpful than these ceremonies might have been the herbs and drugs which the Medicine Man also administered.

To gain and maintain his position of supremacy over enemies inside and outside the tribe, a Sagamo, like Membertou, had to be shrewd and crafty. No doubt it was one of these enemies, jealous of his friendship with the French, who told Champlain that Membertou was "the worst and most treacherous man of his tribe." Hearing from another chief that Membertou was about to attack the French, Poutrincourt sent a few of his men to invite Membertou to the settlement. Without hesitation, Membertou, alone and unescorted, accompanied the messengers, thus proving that the charges were false. When the visit was over, Poutrincourt gave the old man a bottle of wine, which he liked because he said it made him sleep soundly and forget his troubles.

Except for these incidents, it seems that Membertou was trusted and respected by the settlers. On his visits to Port Royal, he was always invited to join the leaders at the table, where they enjoyed his company. Grave and reserved as befitted his position of Great Sagamo, he considered himself the equal of the French Sagamo, Poutrincourt, and expected to be greeted with salvos of guns on his return from a long voyage. He was generous with gifts of valuable furs to the French leader, and Poutrincourt was equally generous to him in return. On one occasion, Membertou asked and received from Poutrincourt a beautiful piece of French cloth in which to wrap the body of a slain leader.

Several stories are told of occasions when Membertou showed his concern for his French friends. One day his keen eyes saw a strange ship far on the horizon, and fearing that it might be an enemy vessel, he burst into the French settlement where a few men were eating their noon meal. Raving at them for sitting there dining when an enemy might be approaching, he rushed out with his daughter to his canoe and paddled off to see for himself who the newcomers might be. To his relief, he found that they were Frenchmen returning to Port Royal. In 1607, when all the settlers were recalled to France for three years, Poutrincourt left the habitation in Membertou's charge. On their return, the French were pleased to see that the chief had harvested and stored the grain and even kept the sticks of furniture intact.

We know of only one occasion when Membertou led a war party against his enemies. The occasion was a war of revenge against the Saco Indians who had killed his son-in-law. Throughout the winter, messengers were sent out to Membertou's allies, while the old Sagamo prepared his strategy and made great speeches to the assembled braves. Finally, on July 6, a great flotilla of canoes set off on the war path. After a fierce battle with great losses on both sides, Membertou and his men returned victorious to Port Royal just as the French were about to sail across the Atlantic for home. Instead of leaving as they had intended, the French remained an extra day in order to hear about the battle exploits of Membertou and his braves, and to celebrate their victory.

One of the reasons for the French presence in Acadia was to convert the natives to the Catholic religion. From the start, the settlers had told Membertou and his men about some of the Christian beliefs. No doubt the Indians, who were always a very courteous audience, listened quietly to the strange stories about hell and heaven and prayers and commandments. Though they themselves had no particular creed, they believed in a great spirit which united man and nature and bound together all living creatures. To them, the after-life was neither a beautiful paradise full of angels, nor a burning place of eternal torment but another hunting ground where spirits could live with their ancestors – which is why they placed kettles and clothes and weapons over the graves of the dead.

When Poutrincourt returned to Port Royal on July 17, 1610, after a three year absence, he brought along Fr. Jessé Fléché, who was to give the Mic Macs their final "lessons" and baptize them in the Christian faith. What the good priest was able to convey in one week is difficult to say. In any case, at the end of that time Membertou and 20 of his people became Christian – or at least were baptized. Among the converts, was the chief's son together with his two wives! With Poutrincourt as godfather, Membertou acquired the name of Henri, after the King of France, Henry IV. His son was called Louis, after Louis XIII; and his wife was called Marie, after the French queen. After confessing his sins, Membertou renounced his role of medicine man and substituted the cross for the sorcerer's bag that he had worn around his neck. What he thought about the new religion or what he really understood about the whole proceedings is not recorded. However, he was so anxious that others should follow his example that he offered to make war on anyone who refused!

The winter after the ceremony, a message came to the French settlement that Membertou was very ill and wished to see Poutrincourt. Braving the ten miles to the wilderness where the Mic Macs had pitched their camps, the Frenchman set out with an Indian guide for Membertou's bedside. On entering the tent he saw the old man lying dressed in his best furs awaiting his death, while members of the tribe stood around him chanting stories of his great deeds. It was the custom among nomadic tribes for

the very old and infirm to fast until they died in order not to become a burden on the other hunters. It seems, however, that Membertou was not quite ready to accept his death, so Poutrincourt took him to Port Royal, put him in front of a warm fire and saw that he was nursed back to health. Poutrincourt also agreed to allow Membertou to be buried with his native ancestors instead of in the Christian cemetery.

Later, when Membertou knew that his death was really approaching, he came back to Port Royal with his wife and some followers. This time Poutrincourt was back in France and the lenient Father Fléché had been replaced by a Jesuit priest who was more strict about Christian regulations. When Membertou reminded Poutrincourt's son Biencourt of his father's promise about the native burial, Father Biard refused to allow such a thing. The old man pleaded with the priest, saying that the Mic Macs would not come to Port Royal after his death, for they disliked passing by a burial ground. However, when he saw that Father Biard was adamant, Membertou gave in. With his dying breath, he exhorted his men to remain friendly with the French and he begged Biencourt to look after his wife and family.

When the old Sagamo finally breathed his last breath, Biencourt kept a vigil over his body throughout the night. The following day, Membertou was buried with all due ceremony, his cross and his bow and arrow over his grave. Afterward, a funeral feast was prepared for the family of the venerable chieftain, the first native person to be baptized in Canada.

Chapter Three

Kondiaronk

Kondiaronk, known to the French as "Le Rat," was the greatest Huron chief of his day. He was a brave and clever man, crafty as a fox when the welfare of his people was at stake. The longer he lived, the greater was his desire for peace and he lived to see his dream come true.

Kondiaronk was born in 1649, a fateful year for the Huron nation. That year, and the following one, the Iroquois swooped down on the Huron villages near Georgian Bay and levelled them to the ground. The panic-stricken survivors abandoned their homeland and fled in all directions. Some took refuge with the French or with neighboring tribes. Others roamed the wilderness to the north and the west.

After years of flight and homelessness, Kondiaronk's tribe, accompanied by the Jesuit priest, Fr. Jacques Marquette, settled at Michilimackinac on the north shore of the Mackinac Straits. On the rising land close to the water, they built a village and surrounded it with wooden pallisades. Inside the palings, they constructed dome-shaped huts with sleeping platforms like upper-berths on a train. Each family had its own little compartment separated from the others by bark and skin. Down the centre of the hut was a passage with a fire for every two families and an opening in the roof the length of the house to allow the smoke to escape. On a nearby hill, enclosed in a stockade, stood the Jesuit mission house and church.

The waters around Michilimackinac teamed with fish. Even in winter they could be caught without effort through holes in the ice. On patches of level ground close to the village, the women sowed corn, peas, beans, and pumpkin.

Shortly after the Hurons' arrival in Michilimackinac, an Ottawa tribe came and settled nearby in their own pallisaded village. The two tribes managed to live side by side without major disputes, but they were never the best of friends. They belonged to two different nations with different customs and languages.

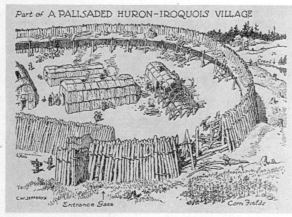
Part of a palisaded Huron-Iroquois Village.
Etching by C.W. Jefferys.

The Hurons and the Iroquois came from the same stock, although they had been quarrelling for years. The Ottawas belonged to the Algonquin nation and were not nearly so advanced as the Iroquois.

Ever since the destruction of their homelands in 1649, the Hurons did their best not to provoke a quarrel with their Iroquois cousins. Their best was not enough. About 10 years after settling in their new home at Michilimackinac, the Hurons got drawn into a quarrel with the powerful nation. Originally, the dispute was between the Iroquois and the Ottawa. An Iroquois chief was murdered in an Ottawa village and the Iroquois vowed to avenge his death. As Kondiaronk well knew, an attack on the Ottawa would likely spill over into the Huron village.

The dispute could not have come at a worse time. South of Michilimackinac, the Iroquois were already on the warpath. Shortly before, the explorer La Salle had built fur-trading posts in the Illinois country and encouraged many western tribes to settle nearby. This move was a blow to the Iroquois because it cut off their access to western furs. Game was scarce in the Iroquois country, and the nation had come to depend on the English trade goods which beaver skins could buy.

Not surprisingly, the Iroquois turned their thoughts to war. In the summer of 1680, they invaded the Illinois country and reduced it to a desert. With this victory behind them, they were spoiling for more conquests. The murder of their chief was as good a reason as any to attack Michilimackinac. To placate the Iroquois, Kondiaronk sent them a wampum (or peace) belt on behalf of his tribe, but to no avail. The Iroquois vowed to have their revenge.

In hot haste, delegates from the Ottawa and the Huron set out for Quebec to seek help from Governor Frontenac. Kondiaronk was the spokesman for the Ottawa.

Both parties had different stories to tell. "Father, take pity on us for we are dead men," said the Ottawa spokesman. Then he went on to accuse the Hurons of treachery. According to him, Kondiaronk had tried to make a separate peace treaty with the Iroquois at the expense of the Ottawa. Kondiaronk denied the accusation. He admitted sending the belt but he denied any treacherous intentions. Frontenac listened to their stories but promised nothing. They were advised to return to their homes and try to keep the peace.

That same year, Frontenac was recalled to France and Governor Le Febvre de la Barre was appointed to succeed him. In the spring, the new governor set out on a campaign against the Iroquois. On the way, his troops were struck down with fever and La Barre was forced to make peace. The Iroquois dictated their own terms. They agreed not to attack the French, but they refused to make peace with the western tribes.

Kondiaronk was disgusted with the treaty. He and his allies saw themselves abandoned to the mercy of their old enemies. Ever since Champlain came to Canada, the Hurons had taken the French side. They had sold their furs at French trading posts. They had acted as guides to French traders and had accepted French priests in their midst. Now, in Kondiaronk's opinion, they were left to fend for themselves.

Meanwhile, La Barre was recalled to France for his bungling and Governor Denonville was sent to Quebec to replace him with instructions to humble the Iroquois. Kondiaronk agreed to ally himself with the new governor on condition that the Iroquois would be brought to their knees. He wanted no peace that excluded his own people.

In 1688, Kondiaronk set off with 100 braves to raid Iroquois territory. On his way, he stopped off at Fort Frontenac for news of the war. There was nothing but bad news awaiting him. The war was over and Iroquois ambassadors were already on their way to Montreal to sign a peace treaty with the French. Kondiaronk was told to return home at once with his warriors. Any attack on the Iroquois would only provoke the anger of the Governor.

Kondiaronk was furious. He believed that he had been duped again. In his opinion, a French-Iroquois alliance could only have one result. Free from the threat of a French attack, the Iroquois would unleash their full fury on the Hurons and their allies.

The wily Kondiaronk concealed his anger and left the fort. Instead of returning home, he devised a clever scheme. He and his warriors returned to their canoes and paddled across Lake Ontario to La Famine, near present-day Oswego, New York. He knew that the Iroquois ambassadors would have to pass that way on their way to Montreal.

For four or five days he and his men lurked in the forest until they spied the Iroquois canoes. Then the Hurons edged close to the landing stage and concealed themselves in the bushes. When the unsuspecting Iroquois disembarked, Kondiaronk pounced. In the confusion, an Iroquois chief was killed, others were wounded and the rest taken prisoner, except one man who managed to escape and make his way to Fort Frontenac to tell the story.

As soon as the prisoners were safely bound, Kondiaronk gave his reasons for the attack. He claimed that Governor Denonville was the master-mind behind the whole ruse. Teganissorens, a respected Iroquois chief, protested that his people were on a peace mission. Pretending to be upset, Kondiaronk vowed vengence on the Governor for having used him to commit such an appalling crime. Then he ordered the men to be set free: "Go home to your country. Though there is war between us, I give you back your liberty. Onontio (the Governor) has made me do so black a deed that I shall never be happy again until your five tribes take a just revenge."

As a sign of his good faith, he presented the Iroquois with guns and ammunition and sent all of the Iroquois, except one man, on their way home. According to Indian custom, this one man would be held prisoner to replace one of Kondiaronk's men who lost his life in the skirmish. The Iroquois were glad to get off with their lives and swore to keep peace with the Hurons.

Well pleased with his ruse, Kondiaronk gathered his men together and paddled back with all possible speed across the lake. On reaching Fort Frontenac, Kondiaronk went in and gloated to the commander: "I have killed the peace. We will see how the Governor will get out of this business."

Back in Michilimackinac, he presented the Iroquois prisoner to the French commander at the fort who knew nothing about the truce. The unfortunate prisoner told his side of the story, but nobody believed him. Instead, he was mocked as a coward for trying to save his own skin and then shot.

Kondiaronk's trickery didn't stop there. He had one more plan to drive a wedge between the Iroquois and the French. Sending for an Iroquois slave who had spent years with the Hurons, and who had seen the execution, he told the man to return to his people and report what he had seen and heard: "Tell them, that the French are only pretending to make peace. They are taking prisoners and killing them."

Whether the Iroquois believed Kondiaronk's stories or not is hard to say. Another act of real treachery on the part of the French took place shortly afterward and that in itself was enough to set the Iroquois on the warpath. A few years earlier, King Louis of France had requested the Canadian governor to send Iroquois prisoners to work on French galley ships. To his credit, Governor La Barre ignored the request. Denonville was more compliant. Some peaceful Iroquois were captured near Fort Frontenac and then bound to the stake. The unfortunate men lamented that they were betrayed without cause in spite of all the care they had always taken in supplying the fort with fish and deer. Their pleas were in vain and they were shipped to France. For native people accustomed to fresh air and freedom, the dark, cramped galleys were like deathtraps. Of the 36 prisoners, only 13 survived.

Iroquois Chieftain (1757-1810)
National Archives of Canada, 0082

The incident enraged the Iroquois. In the following year, they wreaked a terrible revenge on the colony. A large band of men swooped down on the village of Lachine near Montreal, killing and looting all before them. Meanwhile, war broke out in Europe between France and England and spilled over into North America.

After Lachine, Kondiaronk was more convinced than ever that French power was on the wane. Without openly turning against his old allies, he began to send out peace feelers to the Iroquois. When the new Governor, Frontenac, complained, Kondiaronk stood his ground. The French themselves did the same thing, he said. The Hurons had to look out for their own welfare.

As the war dragged on, prices of the trade goods at Michilimackinac grew higher and higher. Another Huron chief, Le Baron, went to Quebec and complained bitterly about the high prices. South of the border, English goods were better and cheaper. The disgruntled Le Baron gathered 30 families around him and settled with the Iroquois near Albany, New York but Kondiaronk refused to join him. In spite of Iroquois promises, he was still wary of his old enemies.

The following year he was at open warfare with them. In order to extend their hunting grounds, the Iroquois made plans to attack the Miami tribe. Kondiaronk warned the Miami of the proposed attack. Then at the head of a small Huron force, he ambushed the invaders and soundly defeated them.

Later that year, the war between France and England came to an end. With the signing of the Treaty of Ryswick, the two European powers agreed to cease hostilities in North America. The native people were also tired of war. They had lost many of their best men in the conflict without gaining anything for themselves.

It took a few years before a final settlement was reached. In the middle of the negotiations, Frontenac died and was replaced by Governor Callière. The new governor was a clever negotiator. After much bickering, all the tribes came together for a meeting in Montreal in 1700. The Iroquois were loud in their complaints against the French, but Kondiaronk made a strong plea for peace: "Let it not be in a forced or insincere way that you ask him [Callière] for peace. For my part, I return to him the hatchet and lay it at his feet." Before the meeting was over, the Iroquois promised to bury the hatchet as well. It was another year before the final treaty was signed. In the meantime, Kondiaronk spared no efforts to get all the western tribes together. It took all his eloquence to persuade them to put aside their suspicions and come to Montreal for discussions.

In the summer, Kondiaronk, accompanied by over 700 delegates, paddled down to Montreal where he was received with a salvo of guns. Discussions got off to a shaky start. The stumbling block was the return of the prisoners-of-war. Kondiaronk had rounded up all the Iroquois prisoners, but the Iroquois came almost empty-handed, claiming that their prisoners were either dead or unwilling to return to their former homes. This was too much for Kondiaronk. With some difficulty, Callière calmed him down by promising to attend to the matter later.

On August 1, Kondiaronk got up for his final speech. Addressing each tribe in turn, he spoke to them of the great need for peace and the advantages it would bring to all. Then, turning to Callière, he implored the Governor to be fair and trustworthy in his dealing with the native people. In the middle of his speech, he fell ill and was placed on an armchair. Offered some wine to strengthen him, he declined in favor of a syrup of maiden-hair fern. In a faltering voice, he completed his address after which he received tremendous applause.

His condition steadily worsened and he had to be carried to the hospital where he died the following morning. His death was mourned by French and Indian alike. The body lay in state for a few days and the Intendant sprinkled holy water over it. Then 60 Iroquois marched in solemn procession to the body and sat in a circle around it while a chanter intoned the traditional Iroquois lament. Tears were shed and the Hurons were presented with gifts to console them for the loss of their chief.

To show their respect for Kondiaronk, the French held a magnificent funeral the following day. Heading the procession was a military escort of 60 soldiers, followed by 16 Huron braves in long beaver robes, their faces blackened and their guns reversed. Then came the clergy and six war chiefs carrying the bier all strewn with flowers. Behind the coffin were Kondiaronk's brothers and sisters accompanied by Huron and Ottawa warriors.

At the end of the service there were two volleys of musketry and a third when the body was lowered into the earth. Kondiaronk was buried in the church in Montreal. On his tomb these words were inscribed: "Here lies the Rat, a Huron chief."

No trace of his grave remains today. The old cathedral is long gone and Kondiaronk's bones lie underneath the present Place d'Armes in Montreal.

Chapter Four

Pontiac

On September 8, 1760, the English flag, the red cross of St. George, was hoisted over the ramparts of Montreal. Canada had changed hands. After more than 150 years, the French regime was over. All that remained to be done was to take over the French forts in the interior, or so the English thought. Little did they know that the native people would fight them every step of the way.

The leader of the revolt was Pontiac, an Ottawa war chief. Because the native people kept no written records, we know very little about Pontiac's early life. He was born about 1720, probably in the Ottawa village near the present-day city of Detroit. Most people say that one of his parents was an Ottawa and the other came from a friendly neighboring tribe.

At that time, the Ottawas lived in three separate villages on the Michigan peninsula. One settlement was at Michilimackinac, another at Saginaw Bay, and the third beside the French Fort Pontchartrain, later knows as Fort Detroit. For many years, the Ottawas had been allies of the French. The first time we read about them is in the writings of Samuel de Champlain. While he was exploring the lands near Georgian Bay, he met a band of Ottawas gathering blueberries. He named them "Cheveux Releves" ("Raised Hair") because they groomed their hair to make it stand straight upwards on the front of the head. According to him, they were traders and fishermen, and cultivated corn and other crops: "They are great people for feasts. They gave us good cheer and received us very kindly."

For several years, the Ottawas controlled the western fur trade. The more they traded with the French, the more they began to depend on the Frenchman's goods. The hatchets, knives and kettles were far superior to their own stone and wooden utensils. Ammunition began to replace the bow and arrow, and in time, the native hunters lost their skill with these weapons. They even acquired a taste for French clothes, especially warm woolen blankets, which they often wore over their shoulders in winter. Worst of all, they acquired a taste for French brandy. Like other native people, they sometimes went for long periods without food and then ate a huge meal. Unused to the new drink, they used it in the same way. They regarded alcohol almost as a kind of magic because it gave them great powers of speech.

Although they liked the French goods, the Ottawas held on to many of their old customs and beliefs. They believed in a universal power or "Great Spirit," and in other lesser spirits that lived in the air, on land, in streams and in lakes. They paid great attention to dreams, because spirits were believed to visit them in dreams. To the disappointment of the French priests, the Ottawas paid little heed to the Christian religion. Once, when a priest was preaching about the death of Christ on the cross a native person spoke up: "White people, we had no part in this matter or this great crime in killing your God. You white people must make restitution yourselves." The Ottawas were often rude to the priests, but this rudeness was probably to prevent the priests and their French friends from coming to the

Ottawa villages and bringing the European diseases to them. The natives could see for themselves the havoc caused by measles, smallpox and tuberculosis.

There was no great chief over all the Ottawa nation. The unit was the band, ranging from a few families to a few hundred. Sometimes the leaders of the local bands would unite together under one outstanding chief like Pontiac. The chief was not an absolute ruler who could force others to do his will. He was a respected man who could lead and advise his people. Because of their nomadic life, there was no great cohesion among members of the tribes. Each man was his own master, free to follow the war chief or not, and to return to his village at his own wish. A chief like Pontiac had to be daring and resourceful, with a gift of oratory to inspire his followers and bend them to his will.

When he was a young boy, Pontiac was no doubt brought up like other children of his tribe. Among the native people, children, especially boys, were very much loved and cherished. When the infant was about six months old, the parents held a great feast in his honor. At the gathering, the medicine man offered prayers to the child's guardian spirit. Then he took a bodkin and awl from his medicine pouch and pierced the child's ears and nose. A little quill was inserted in the hole in the nose and tiny slivers of bark in the ears. Later on, when the wounds were healed, colored beads were placed in the ears and a bright ornamental stone in the nose, The ceremony ended with a feast, after which the mother handed out gifts such as furs or kettles to the guests.

For the first few years of his life, Pontiac spent most of his time in his cradle board, a stout wooden plank with a strong bar across the top to protect his face and a little shelf at the bottom where he could rest his feet. Since he was the son of a chief, the cradle was probably adorned with many beads and bells, as well as one of his father's bows. The cradle board was packed with moss or down to keep him dry and warm. At the back of the board was a leather carrying strap which the mother placed across her forehead or around her shoulders. Sometimes the board was laid on the ground or hung by its strap on a nearby tree. When the child cried, his mother would sing him a song that described the duties of a young boy.

At the age of three, the child was weaned and began to eat regular food, chewed up for him by his mother. Later he was allowed out of the cradle and given a little bow and a stiff straw arrow to play with. As he got older, he was allowed to practice with very light, real arrows. Like the other young boys, he had few or no tasks to do. By day he ran races, wrestled and played games like "snow snake." This game was played with a wooden rod about three feet long, the head raised slightly like the

head of a snake. The object of the game was to see who could slide the rod the farthest over the smooth snow.

A baby in a cradle board.
Reprinted, by permission, Glenbow
Archives: NA-1406-99

For Pontiac there was no such thing as formal school. Native children learned how to hunt and fish and survive in the woods by listening to their elders and by imitating them. When he was 8 or 10-years-old, the young boy began hunting birds and squirrels. Wrestling, foot racing and canoe racing gave him the chance to test his strength and improve his skills. In the evening, he listened to stories by the fireside which passed on the wisdom and lore of his tribe. These tales placed great value on courage, endurance and generosity.

Throwing the Snow Snake.
Etching by C.W. Jefferys.

In the summer, young Pontiac probably wore no clothes at all. To protect his skin from the flies and mosquitoes, his mother smeared his body with animal grease. In the winter, he wore breeches and leather moccasins and a tunic of the same material. At puberty the boy went into the woods and fasted, sometimes for a few days. During the fast he was expected to dream about a spirit (or manitou) who would be his own special guardian for the rest of his life. Very likely

Pontiac had a likeness of the manitou tatooed on his body. When the boy killed his first game, it was an important occasion for he was now a hunter who could support a family of his own. To mark the occasion, his parents gave a feast at which the animal was cooked and everyone was given a piece of the meat.

While Pontiac was growing up, the Ottawas around Detroit lived in dome-shaped huts about 100 feet long, 24 feet wide and 20 feet high. To make these huts, long, slender poles were driven deep into the ground, and curved and tied at the top. Around these poles were wooden cross-pieces and the whole structure was covered with strips of fur, woven mats, or pieces or bark. "It is certain," says Cadillac, the first French commander at Detroit, "that their huts are weatherproof and no rain whatever gets into them." There was an opening at each end of the building covered by a flap and another one at the top to allow the smoke to escape.

When Pontiac and his family went on their winter hunt, they lived in small teepees. Built much the same way as the large building, the teepees were so small that the people had to sleep in a crouched position. When the family had to move, they rolled up the covers of the teepee leaving the poles behind, because it was easier to find suitable poles in the woods than to take them to the new site. In the teepee and in the larger dwelling, the floor was bare earth or snow covered with branches, rush mats or animal skin.

Every year the lives of Pontiac and the other Ottawas followed the same pattern. When winter came they set out from the village on their winter hunt, usually in small family groups. Even a great chief endured the hardships of the hunt. Indeed, one of the reasons he was elected chief was because of his skill in the chase. After finding a suitable hunting ground, the group pitched their teepee and the men set out to shoot and trap bears, foxes, deer, elk and other game.

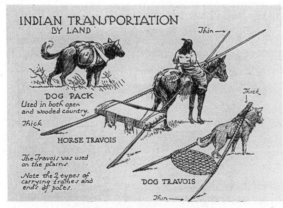

Indian transportation

As the white man moved farther inland, the animals fled deeper into the wilderness and game became scarcer and scarcer.

Sometimes the men trudged for whole days in bitter cold and blinding snow without making a single catch. In the evening, they made their weary way back to the camp, stopping now and then to grub for food under the blanket of snow. When game was plentiful, they dragged the animals home and shared food equally with all. While the men hunted, the women dried the meat and prepared the furs for market.

In early spring, they returned to Detroit, their canoes laden with furs, bear oil and the sap they collected from the maple trees. In May, the men took the furs to the fort and bartered them for clothing, kettles, hoes and other trade goods. Meanwhile, the women and the men too old to hunt, planted corn, peas, beans, pumpkins and other vegetables. Later in the spring, the men went fishing and hunting for small game, but these trips were for shorter periods and closer to home.

Summer was a time of rest and pleasure. In the open fields around the camp, men would sit in the sunshine playing games of chance like the game of straws or the dice game. A game they particularly enjoyed was lacrosse. One writer says that they liked it so much "they will give up their food and drink not only to play it, but to watch the game." The foot races between the Ottawas and the French at Detroit were famous all over the west. The Ottawas also loved to dance. There were strawberry dances, green corn dances, fire dances and medicine dances which might go all night.

A lacrosse match
Reprinted, by permission, Glenbow
Archives, NA-11406-121

Summer was also the the time for court-ship and marriage. Although there was no law against polygamy, a wife and husband usually stayed together if they had children. Pontiac was probably married when he was around 20-years-old. According to accounts he had three wives, although it is not known whether he had more than one wife at the same time. He had at least two sons.

Everyone agrees that Pontiac had the proud and haughty bearing of a man accustomed to respect. As a war chief, he was strong and muscular and his frame was well filled out. According to one writer he was tall but not handsome. Another writer says he was remarkably good-looking and careful of his dress and appearance. In the fashion of the Ottawas, his short black hair was worn straight upright and adorned with colored feathers. Around his neck he probably had a collar of white plumes and his ears and nose were adorned with brightly colored beads. A likeness of his personal guardian spirit was probably tatooed on his chest and his whole body gleamed from the bear grease used to protect it from mosquitoes.

All his life, Pontiac had been an ally of the French even though the English tried to lure him away. It must have been a shock to him when the English defeated the French and took control of the country in 1760. To the native people, however, one group of white men in the forts was very much like another. If the conquerors respected his people's rights, Pontiac was willing to do business with them.

Shortly after the fall of Montreal, the English commander, Sir Jeffrey Amherst, sent out an army to raise the British flag over the western forts. The leader of the expedition was Major Robert Rogers of New England, a well-known Indian fighter. Under his command, he had over 200 soldiers, known as "Roger's Rangers," men who were well used to wilderness warfare. Amherst expected no trouble. He despised the native people. In his own words, they were "only fit to live with the inhabitants of the woods, being more nearly allied to the brute than to human creation."

At the end of November, the boats carrying Rogers and his Rangers sailed up the Detroit River. On the west side of the river loomed Fort Pontchartrain, with the French flag, the fleur de lis, still flying over the ramparts. Founded in 1701 by La Mothe Cadillac, the great fort was about 3/4 of a mile in circumference and surrounded by wooden pallisades. Inside the fort, there were about 70 or 80 houses with long sloping roofs and dormer windows, as well as a Catholic church and soldiers' barracks. The streets were narrow, being only about 10 feet wide. Between the houses and the pallisade there was a wide passage all around the fort called the "chemin du ronde," or "the circle road."

Outside the fort, for about 10 miles on each side, were the houses of the French settlers. Like their friends in Quebec they built their homes close together on the riverbank, their long narrow farms stretching back two or three miles. The snug homes were made of log, sometimes painted white, with thatched roofs and picket fences in front. Each settler had a vegetable garden and an orchard but most of the land was uncultivated because the people were fur traders not farmers.

They were cheerful people who loved to dance and make merry. If they couldn't afford French wine, they made their own from the wild grapes that grew abundantly around Detroit. They were on good terms with the native people, attended their dances and joined in their sports. Almost everyone knew at least one native language.

There were three native villages on the outskirts of the settlement. On the west side of the river, a few miles below the fort, were the lodges of the Potawatomis. Opposite them, on the east side, was the Huron village, with the Ottawas a few miles farther north.

On November 29, Rogers and his men, dressed in green buckskins and green berets, marched smartly into the fort and made their way to the main square. Lined up to surrender their arms was the French garrison. As groups of settlers stood sadly by, the fleur de lis was lowered to the ground and the English flag hoisted in its place. Detroit was in English hands.

At first, everything went smoothly. A New Englander, George Croghan, who knew the native people and their ways, held meetings with Pontiac and the other chiefs. In his speeches, he painted the future in rosy colors. Before long, he said, English traders would arrive at the fort with better and cheaper trade goods. Pontiac, and the other chiefs were well pleased with Croghan's words.

At the same meeting, the chiefs asked that a doctor and a gunsmith be sent to the fort. Then they made one ominous statement. They reminded Croghan that the British had promised "that this country was given by God to the Indians and that you would preserve it for our joint use." Like most European countries, the British believed that nomadic people had no rights of ownership and so they had no intention of keeping that promise.

Shortly afterwards, Croghan and Rogers departed, leaving Captain Donald Campbell in temporary command. He was a sensible man who did his best to get along with the natives and the French settlers. Almost immediately he was faced with a major dilemma. During the French regime, it was customary for the commander of the fort to give ammunition and other presents to the native people. These gifts were not considered as bribes but as a kind of rent for the use of native land. Besides, ever since the Europeans set foot in the new world, each side gave the other presents, just as diplomats do the world over. Among the native people, gift giving was also very common. On his own initiative, Campbell handed out what little ammunition and presents he could spare. He was well aware, however, that the practice would soon have to stop because General Amherst was completely against it.

Like the other native people, Pontiac went out hunting in the winter of 1760. In the spring, the hunters returned to the fort to exchange their furs for trade goods. To their dismay they found that the goods they wanted were in short supply and prices were higher than expected. Besides, no rum was for sale.

The first signs of trouble came not from Detroit but from the Seneca Indians to the east. For years this tribe had fought on the English side. Now, instead of the rewards they expected, they discovered that some of their homelands were being granted to English settlers. Justly angry, they sent messengers to Detroit asking the tribes to unite in fighting the English, but the plot was discovered.

Very soon Pontiac was grumbling about the high prices and the lack of rum and presents. Also, like the other chiefs, he could see that the English despised him and his people. Where formerly the native people were welcome at the fort, they were now mocked and insulted. The free and easy camaraderie of the French was replaced by coldness and suspicion on the part of the newcomers.

Other elements came together to stir up the native people. Although the English had conquered Canada, the war between them and the French was still raging in Europe and a short time previously, the Spanish had entered the war on the side of France. This raised the hopes of some of the French settlers in Canada. If the English were to be defeated in Europe, might they not be driven from Canada as well? Some French settlers allowed themselves to hope and encouraged Pontiac and his people to do the same.

Noble Indian of the Ottawa Nation
Reprinted, by permission, National
Archives of Canada: 0082

At this critical time, encouragement came from another quarter as well. In a neighboring tribe, a preacher arose who became known as "the Delaware Prophet."

The prophet told his audiences that the Maker of Life had appeared to him in a vision and given him a message for his people. They were to return to their old ways and stop relying on the white man. Excessive drinking and other vices they had learned from the white man should cease: "As to those who came to trouble your land, drive them out, make war upon them. I do not like them at all; they know me not. They are my enemies and the enemies of your brothers. . . ." Pontiac was impressed with the message. If he could get the tribes to unite, they might be able to drive the English out of the country.

On April 27, 1763, he called a historic meeting on the Ecorse River about 10 miles below the fort. Besides the Ottawas, delegates from the Potawatomi and the non-Christian Hurons turned out to hear him. In a fiery speech, he urged the 500 warriors to follow the advice of the Delaware Prophet and drive "the dogs dressed in red" (the English soldiers) out of Detroit. With one voice the warriors shouted their agreement.

A plan was agreed on. In four days Pontiac and a group of his followers would go to the fort to dance the calumet dance. Once there, they would use the occasion to spy out the land.

On May 1, Pontiac and 40 or 50 men crossed the Detroit river in their slender birch bark canoes. One by one, they filed through the gate of the fort until they reached the space opposite Captain Campbell's house. Then they began their calumet dance.

Indians dancing at the fort.
Reprinted, by permission,
Glenbow Archives: NA-843-34

The calumet, or peace pipe, was made of polished red stone drilled into a hollow wooden stem about two feet long adorned with colored feathers. It was held aloft to the sun while the men danced in a ring pretending to attack each other, but when they touched the calumet the mock battle was over. All the while the warriors chanted and danced to the music of Indian drums.

While the English gathered around to watch the dance, some of Pontiac's men melted away to check the number of soldiers and the position of the storehouse. The dance over, the native people prepared to depart, promising to return in a few days to give another display. None the wiser, the commander, Henry Gladwyn, distributed a few presents and the natives left.

Well pleased with his ruse, Pontiac called another council meeting in the council house of the Potawatomis. To ensure secrecy, sentinels were placed at the doors and women were forbidden to enter. One hundred chiefs from the Ottawa, Potawatomi and Huron tribes sat in circles around the tribal fire when Pontiac arose to speak.

The speech was a rousing one. He said in part:

> It is important for us my brothers that we exterminate from our lands this nation which seeks only to destroy us. . . . The English sell us goods twice as dear as the French do and their goods do not last. . . . When I go to see the English commander and say to him that some of our comrades are dead, instead of bewailing their death as the French do, he laughs at me and at you. If I ask anything for our sick he refuses with the reply that he has no use for us. . . . Therefore my brothers, we must swear their destruction. . . . I have sent messages to our brothers the Chippewas of Saginaw and to our brothers the Ottawas of Michilimackinac and to those of the Thames River to join us. . . .

At the end of the speech he unveiled his latest plan. In two days time, he and his principal chiefs with guns hidden under their blankets, would enter the fort and ask for a meeting with Gladwyn and his officers. At a signal from Pontiac, the chiefs would take out their weapons and kill the unsuspecting men. Upon hearing the shots, the native people in the streets would fall on the remaining troops.

To the native people there was nothing disgraceful about such actions. This was war and the English were the enemy. In war it was permissible to use any tactics that might vanquish the enemy with the least loss of native lives. Sir Jeffrey Amherst was not above treachery of a different kind, when he suggested to one of his commanders that a way be found to spread the deadly smallpox disease among another tribe.

Unfortunately for Pontiac, his plot was a failure. Gladwyn got wind of the story and he made his own plans.

On the morning of May 7, the gates of the fort were open as usual. At 10 o'clock, Pontiac and his men, their weapons concealed under their blankets, filed along the river road and made their way through the entrance. Inside the gate they were surprised to find the sentinels armed to the teeth. Nevertheless, they pressed on. The streets of the fort were unnaturally quiet, stores were closed, and the soldiers on the parade ground were lined up on guard, their weapons gleaming in the sun. The majority of the native people slipped away as planned and Pontiac with his chiefs made their way to the council chamber.

Inside sat Captain Campbell and Major Gladwyn, their pistols in their belts. Pontiac paused for a moment. Then he enquired why all the "young chiefs" were absent and why so many men were standing armed in the streets. Gladwyn smoothly replied that the men were armed to preserve discipline in case of an unfriendly act, but he assured Pontiac that no treachery was expected from the friendly Ottawa.

For a moment, Pontiac was taken aback. He was not fooled. He was too clever for that. He guessed that the plot had been discovered and that his plan would have to be changed. Holding a wampum belt in his hand he made a speech about the death of six Ottawa chiefs and he asked Gladwyn for something to soothe the natives' grief. Gladwyn pretended to believe him. As a token of his supposed sympathy, he presented Pontiac with six suits of clothes for the victim's families. Baffled by his prey, the war chief tried to save the situation. He told Gladwyn that he would return in a few days to smoke the peace pipe when all his young men had returned from their winter hunt. On his side, Gladwyn replied that he would receive only the chieftans.

Pontiac making his speech to Captain Campbell.
Etching by C. W. Jefferys.

Outside the fort, Pontiac and his men must have breathed more easily. Since they had not been killed or captured, he probably hoped against hope that the English were ignorant of the whole conspiracy. To impress them with his good intentions he hit on another plan. He invited the French and the native tribes to a friendly game of lacrosse in a field beside the fort. All afternoon the game went on with much noise and excitement, thoughts of treachery apparently far from their minds. In the evening, he called the chiefs of the three tribes together and reported on his meeting with Gladwyn. At the meeting it was decided that he should try again to carry out his plot.

The morning of May 9 dawned calm and clear. It was a Catholic feast day and the Catholic priest Father Bocquet lead his parishioners in procession to a church outside the walls. As they returned to the fort just before 11 o'clock, the sound of their chanting filled the summer air. Suddenly, the commons outside the fort swarmed with native people and Pontiac approached the gates, only to find them barred against him. In a loud voice, he demanded that the gates be opened to him and his braves. Gladwyn sent out a messenger to say that Pontiac and a few of his chiefs could enter, but the rest would not be admitted.

Foiled again, Pontiac went away to plan his next move. His prestige hung in the balance. Stirred up to do battle, his young braves could easily turn against him because of the failed attempts. Back in his village, he put on his warpaint, brandished his tomahawk and danced his war dance. As warrior after warrior joined in the dance, Pontiac urged the men to strike at the English outside the fort and cut off supplies to the garrison. If the soldiers couldn't be killed inside the fort, they would be starved to death. Meanwhile, he had his camp moved across the river to a site about two miles above the fort.

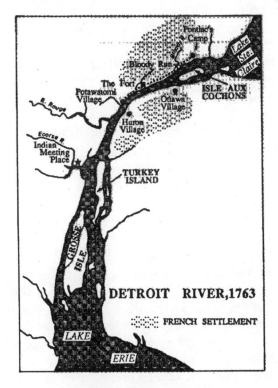

Bloody Run and Pontiac's camp

One war party pounced on an English farmhouse, killed the owners and drove away their cattle. Another party paddled to Île au Couchon (now, Belle Isle) to seize the garrison's cattle. In the attack, they killed the man in charge, Sergeant Fisher, and four others. Pontiac himself took no part in these massacres.

From their new camp at Parent's Creek (now called Bloody Run) the rest of the warriors began firing on the fort. Toward evening, Pontiac received good news from his Chippewa allies. They had heard from Pontiac that a group of 12 English soldiers were on their way to Detroit and on his advice, they had ambushed the men, managing to kill four and taking the rest prisoner.

The following day the siege continued in earnest. For six hours, the native people fired on the fort from behind hills and barns but the English held their ground. Toward evening, Major Gladwyn sent a messenger to Pontiac to see whether a settlement could be reached, but nothing could be agreed on.

In the morning, the fighting resumed without much result. Pontiac grew impatient. The Indians were not used to siege warfare and they knew little about it. They were accustomed to short, swift assaults, not long battles. Though they were brave people, with tremendous endurance, they hated to lose even one warrior.

To speed matters up, Pontiac sent a few French settlers to the fort to discuss a truce. No terms were agreed on, and the siege continued.

When the war was a week old, the French settlers sent a delegation to Pontiac to find out what he had in mind. The settlers were in a tight squeeze. Caught in the middle between the native people and the English, they didn't know where to turn. Many of them would have been glad to see the English driven out, but they were bound by treaty to keep the peace. Meanwhile, the fur trade was in ruins and Pontiac was demanding some of their ammunition and supplies. Pontiac politely told them that the war would soon be over if they threw in their lot with him.

As the siege dragged on, the food supplies at the fort began to run low and Major Gladwyn forced the French settlers to contribute. The native people were short of food too and the French were forced to give to them as well. A delegation of Frenchmen came to Pontiac to voice their complaints and after hearing them out, he promised to punish any thievery on the part of the natives. Then he asked the settlers' permission to raise corn on their unused land. They agreed to his request and that very evening the native women began to plant their corn in French fields.

Meanwhile, outside Detroit, Pontiac's allies were scoring victory after victory. One by one, the western forts fell into native hands. First to fall was Fort Sandusky, followed by Fort St. Joseph, Fort Miami and Fort Ouiatanon. These victories took place

with the help and encouragement of Pontiac and his Ottawas.

Victories were not just confined to the forts. The middle of May, Lieutenant Abraham Cuyler had left Fort Niagara bound for Detroit with 100 soldiers and provisions. His ten boats cruised peacefully across Lake Erie, unaware of the Indian revolt. On May 28, they reached Point Pelée near the mouth of the Detroit River. As the party prepared to set up camp, a force of Hurons from Detroit stole out of the nearby woods and attacked the unsuspecting men. In a panic, the soldiers dropped their arms and rushed to the boats with the Hurons in hot pursuit.

Only two of the boats, carrying about 50 men managed to escape and make their way back to Niagara. The remainder, with the prisoners and stores of provisions, were taken to Detroit. On the morning of May 31, the Detroit garrison spied a convoy of boats bearing the British flag gliding up the river toward the fort. Loud cheers broke out, as the men awaited their approaching friends and badly needed provisions. As the vessels drew nearer, the soldiers' hearts turned to stone – the boats were full of jeering native people.

May gave way to June, and the siege of Detroit dragged on. With so many natives in such close quarter for weeks, and with food supplies dwindling, quarrels began to break out. The attackers had expected an easy victory and they were bitterly disappointed. In a drinking bout, some English prisoners were killed and the Potawatomi became so angry at the atrocity that they went to the fort to sue for peace. Teata, the chief of the Christian Hurons, who had been dragged into the war in the first place, followed suit. The leader of the Chippewa at Sault Ste. Marie, "Le Grande Saultier" as he was called, sent his son to Pontiac to complain about the war chief's behavior. Pontiac was roundly scolded for his harsh treatment of prisoners and his rudeness to the French. Though he was cut to the quick, Pontiac heard the complaints in silence. Great war chief though he was, he had to listen to another chief's criticism.

The following day he set out to placate the French. With two of his men, he made arrangement with the settlers for supplies. He even gave them receipts signed with his mark and it is said that he later paid back the debts.

A few days later, a boat with soldiers and supplies managed to reach the fort. As it sailed past the Huron village, its guns opened fire on the native cabins killing some and wounding others.

Pontiac was alarmed at this turn of events. Now, more than ever, he needed French aid, for without expert help the fort would not be captured. On July 1, he called a meeting with the settlers. Holding a war belt aloft he addressed the nervous audience: "If you are French, accept the belt. If you are English we declare war on you." A settler arose to reply. With a copy of the English-French treaty in his hand, he told Pontiac that the settlers' hands were tied. They sympathized with him, but they were bound to keep the peace. Some of the young men were not in agreement. Picking up the war belt, they threw in their lot with the natives.

Word of the native uprisings was slow to reach New York. When the first news filtered in, Amherst was not very worried. He thought they were isolated rampages – just what he expected from unruly natives. It never entered his mind that the Indians were rational people who might have real grievances. He refused to believe that they had the foresight to join together against the British. Orders were sent out to show native troublemakers no mercy. In the meantime, he hoped for a speedy end to the conflict so that he could return to England in peace.

As the news became more alarming, he was forced to take further action. His aide, Captain James Dayell, was sent to Albany to collect troops and proceed to Fort Niagara. If Dayell thought it necessary, he could then sail to Detroit. On July 28, Dayell reached

Detroit with a contingent of 300 soldiers. Luck was on his side. A dense fog blanketed the river near Detroit and he managed to reach the fort in safety.

Spirits soared in the fort. With the extra men and supplies the garrison could hold out indefinitely. The young Dayell was not content with defensive warfare – he wanted to lead his men outside the fort and strike at the Ottawa camp. In his opinion, English soldiers, well armed and well trained, would make short work of a horde of savages. Gladwyn reluctantly agreed.

In the dead of night on the last day of July, Dayell and 250 soldiers stole quietly out of the fort. Two by two they marched up the river road while two boats glided up the river to their right to join in the the attack. About two miles above the fort the army had to cross a small stream called Parent's Creek. When the first men reached the centre of the wooden bridge, they were met by a hail of fire. Pontiac had been expecting them.

In their confusion the soldiers fired wildly into the darkness. Many of them fell in their tracks and the river ran red with their blood. Dayell urged the survivors to the heights across the river where Pontiac's army was supposed to be entrenched, but the Ottawas had stolen away. Meanwhile, the men to the rear began to make their retreat. But the wily Pontiac was ready for them too. He had split his troops. Half of his army lay in wait behind barricades nearer the fort, where they shot at the retreating soldiers. By 8 o'clock, the remnants of the shattered army managed to reach the protection of the fort and Dayell himself lay dead on the battlefield. From that day on, the creek was named Bloody Run because of the red blood that dyed its waters.

The victory raised the morale of the native people. Messengers were sent to the neighboring tribes and Pontiac's prestige soared.

August saw a temporary lull in the fighting, but Pontiac had another trick up his sleeve. The fort might still be starved out. In early September, a group of Ottawas and Chippewas ambushed an English vessel on Lake Erie, but after bitter fighting they were forced to withdraw. A Seneca attack on an English convoy passing over the Niagara portage was more successful. As a convoy of 25 horses and wagons escorted by 30 soldiers made their way through Devil's Hole, they were set upon by an army of Senecas. The soldiers were trapped. On one side was a huge precipice overlooking Niagara Falls; the other side was bordered by steep wooded cliffs. It was not a battle but a massacre. The terrified horses reared in the air and plunged headlong over the cliffs, dragging men and wagons behind them. Only two men escaped the carnage.

As September gave way to October, the native situation grew more and more desperate. Pontiac and his allies had won many battles and captured many forts, but Detroit and Fort Pitt still stood. Food was running low and ammunition had almost run out. For five months the allies had held together, something almost unheard of in Indian warfare. Now, one by one the tribes began to sue for peace. They could see no hope for a final victory. Besides, they had to go out on their winter hunt, or face starvation.

Pontiac held grimly on. A false rumor reached his ears that a French army was on its way to help him. For the moment, his spirits rose and he called another council meeting together, but many of his allies had lost heart. An early snow blanketed the land making the siege more hopeless.

His dreams of French help were dashed in late October when messengers arrived from Commander Neyon at Fort du Chartres in the Illinois country with news that the French and the English were definitely and finally at peace: "Our hearts are now as one. You cannot strike one nation without having the other for an enemy also." The French settlers got another letter reminding them too to keep the peace.

Neyon's letter must have been a great blow to Pontiac. All along he had been counting on help from his French "brother." Now he had no options left. His own men were deserting him; his cause was lost. What was to become of his people? He, himself, was under a cloud. Weary of war and almost starving, the people who had once rallied to his call might turn against him in his disgrace.

He was forced to give in – at least for the time being. He dictated a letter which was translated and taken to Mayor Gladwyn. In part the letter said:

> The word which my father [Neyon] has sent me to make peace I have accepted. . . . I think you will forget the bad things which have taken place for some time past. Likewise I will forget what you have done to me.

Gladwyn replied that the message would be sent to Amherst, because only the general had the power to grant peace.

Early in November, Pontiac left Detroit, a sad and bitter man. No longer the respected war chief who had inspired his people with hope, he was shunned by many for bringing ruin on their heads. In spite of Neyon's letter, he found it difficult to believe that France was willing to give up the struggle. How could two bitter enemies bury the hatchet so fast? He resolved to go down to Fort du Chartres and find out the truth from the lips of Neyon himself.

With several Ottawa followers, he journeyed toward Illinois country. During the winter, they pitched camp on the Riviere des Miamis (Maumee river) and hunted for food. With the coming of Spring he continued his journey, stirring up several tribes on the way.

When he reached the French fort, Neyon greeted him kindly enough, but he could give him little comfort. Whether he liked it or not, the war was over; at any moment Neyon expected an English army to arrive at the fort and take it over. At a General Council, Pontiac made an eloquent speech imploring the commander to ask the French king not to desert the native people, but Neyon made no promises and Pontiac departed.

In mid-June, Neyon left for France and Captain St. Ange from Vincennes was sent to replace him until the expected arrival of the English. Thinking that the new commander might be more helpful, Pontiac went to see him. All he got for his trouble was a little ammunition for hunting; with that he had to be content.

Gloomy as the situation seemed, in his heart he still had hope. From his village by the Miami River, he began plotting with other native chiefs. He sent a war belt down to the Arkansas Indians urging them to stop the English forces on their way up the Mississippi. According to accounts, he also spread the rumor, which he may have heard from some settlers, that a French army would soon come to the country. His friend, Shawnee chief Kaske, also made his way to Fort du Chartres for help. Turned down, Kaske later went as far as New Orleans to plead with the French governor there, but to no avail.

In his own village, Pontiac began to lose face. Another Ottawa chief named Manitou started to sew discontent among the Ottawas and even persuaded some of them to go to Detroit to sue for peace. The Hurons from Sandusky, once his strongest supporters, also laid down their arms. Early in 1764, the powerful Senecas lost heart. Together with several other tribes, they sent delegates to an English conference at Niagara presided over by Sir William Johnson.

In the summer, Colonel Gage (who had replaced Amhurst as commander-in-chief) sent an army under Colonel Bradstreet to Detroit. Bradstreet was a vain and foolish man. Hoodwinked by a group of native people, he sent one of his officers down the Mississippi to make treaties with tribes that he thought were now on the English side. The choice fell on Captain Thomas Morris. With an escort of two Frenchmen and some native people, Morris set out on his journey. A little way down the Miami River the luckless officer found himself surrounded by hostile Indians. In a few moments he was dragged from his horse and brought face to face with Pontiac.

In a haughty voice, Pontiac asked Morris if he had come to tell lies like the rest of his countrymen. Then he presented Morris with a letter addressed to him from New Orleans. According to the letter, a French army had landed in Louisiana and the English would be driven out of the country. Evidently some of the French were still trying to fool Pontiac into believing that help could be expected from France.

Morris was in a tight spot. At a council meeting, the other chiefs decided to kill him, but Pontiac dissuaded them saying, "We do not put ambassadors to death." Morris believed that Pontiac was weary of fighting. "I will lead the nations to war no more," the chief said. "Let them be at peace if they choose, but I myself will never be a friend of the English. I shall now become a wanderer in the woods and if they come to seek me there while I have an arrow left I will shoot at them." Morris believed that those words were spoken in despair and that Pontiac could easily be won over to the English side. Whatever the reason, the chief allowed Morris to continue his journey and provided him with a belt to ensure his safety through the other native villages.

Pontiac held out for another year, but he was fighting a losing battle. By degrees, his few remaining allies gave up their arms and sued for peace. They could see the writing on the wall. The English were in the forts to stay and the natives would have to submit, or be beaten into submission. In April 1764, Pontiac took one last dramatic step. With a few followers, he made his way to Fort du Chartres in Illinois and burst in on a meeting between the newly arrived English commander, Lieutenant Alexander Fraser, and outgoing French commander, St. Ange de Bellerive. In a loud voice, he demanded that Fraser be imprisoned as an intruder; it seems that he still had hopes of reinforcements from the French.

St. Ange managed to calm him down. The next day he called him to a meeting and laid the facts before him. All the tribes had come to terms, and the French and the English were now like brothers. Help from the French king was completely out of the question. Pontiac gave in at last. "My father," he said to St. Ange, "you urge me so much to make peace that I can no longer refuse you. . . . For the future, we will regard the English as brothers, since you wish to make us all one."

Some of the natives and French settlers around Fort du Chartres still resented Fraser and the English troops. The same old rumors were whispered that France was about to declare war on England. Fraser was in a hornet's nest. Some of the angry native fighters captured him and threatened him with death but Pontiac came to his aid. Fraser admired Pontiac: "He is in a manner adored by all the nations hereabouts, and more remarkable for his integrity and humanity than either Frenchman or Indian in the colony. He has always been as careful of the lives of my men and of my own life as if he had been our father."

After a few false starts, Pontiac and several other chiefs met the English agent, George Croghan, at Fort Ouiatanon and made a formal peace treaty. The war chief made one important condition: the English must not think that by gaining the forts they had also gained the rights to Indian lands. They would not be owners, but tenants as the French had been. As we saw before, the English had no intention of abiding by such a condition.

Accompanied by Pontiac, Croghan pressed on to Detroit for a meeting with the local chiefs. At the council, Pontiac held up the peace pipe and said:

Father, I declare to all nations that I had made my peace with you before I came here; and I now deliver my pipe to Sir William Johnson that he may know that I have made peace and taken the King of England to be my father.

He also agreed to visit Oswego in the spring to conclude an official treaty.

The revolt was over and the country was at peace. After almost three years of fighting, the Union Jack replaced the fleur de lis in the whole country then known as Canada. Beneath the surface there were still rumblings of discontent. English settlers were forging their way west onto lands that the Indians considered to be their hunting grounds. Pontiac and several other chiefs complained to Croghan but their complaints fell on deaf ears. In a few cases, some settlers around Detroit did sign deeds to their lands with Pontiac, but that was all.

George Croghan treated Pontiac with great respect. In a letter to General Gage he said, "Pontiac is a shrewd, sensible Indian of few words, and commands more respect among his own nation than any Indian I ever saw could do among his own tribe." The wily Croghan planned to turn his friendship with Pontiac to English advantage. In another letter he wrote, "I am mistaken if I don't ruin his influence with his own people before I part with him."

Croghan seems to have been partially successful. Some of the chiefs began to be jealous of Pontiac and his new friendship with the English. Fuel was added to the flame when the rumor spread that he was going to receive a pension for life!

The formal treaty was signed at Fort Ontario (now Oswego, New York). It was hot July weather and a green arbor was erected near the fort to shade the assembly from the sun. Sir William Johnson opened the meeting. In solemn silence he lit Pontiac's peace pipe as a sign that all hostilities were over. On the last day of the meeting, Pontiac spoke for all the western tribes: "I take the Great Spirit to witness that what I am going to say I am determined steadfastly to perform. While I had the French king by the hand, I kept a fast hold on it and now having you my father by the hand, I shall do the same in conjunction with all the western nations in my district." He was as good as his word. From that day forward, he remained at peace with the English.

After the conference Pontiac settled in the Ottawa village on the Miami River. Meanwhile, the settlers continued to press their way forward into Indian territory. To make matters worse, these rough frontiersmen often abused and insulted the rightful owners of the land. The unfortunate Indians felt that they had been duped. War belts began to circulate among them and the old stories about a French invasion even began to take hold.

Pontiac found himself in a strange position. He, the great war chief, was calling for peace, while some of his former allies were ready to go on the warpath again. Even members of his own tribe began to turn against him. No longer welcome in the Ottawa village at Detroit, he was also ousted from his new village on the Miami River.

In the winter of 1768, he went to hunt in the Illinois country. While he was there, a quarrel broke out and Pontiac seems to have threatened revenge. The following spring he returned, the dispute apparently forgotten. With his two sons and his few followers he was on his way to Fort du Chartres to sell his furs. Across the river from the fort his old friend St. Ange de Bellerive lived in the settlement at St. Louis, which was in Spanish hands.

Pontiac paid a visit to St. Ange and was received with all kindness. After a few days, he crossed the river to Cahokia (now a suburb of St. Louis), a place full of Illinois Indians of the Peorian tribe who held a grudge against him from the year before. At a council meeting, the tribe hatched a plot to kill Pontiac while he was still among them.

The end came swiftly. On April 20, the unsuspecting Pontiac went into an English store to trade, his only companion a Peorian tribesman who pretended to be his friend. On their way out of the store, the Peorian raised his tomahawk and buried it in

Pontiac's brain.

The English governor at Fort du Chartres gave orders that Pontiac's body be buried respectfully at Cahokia. It is said that St. Ange later had Pontiac's remains taken across the river and interned with military honors in St. Louis.

From the beginning, Pontiac's cause was hopeless. His wilderness warriors were no match for the trained soldiers of the British Empire. Without the expected help from France, he had neither the supplies nor the weapons to hold out. Besides, his own people had become so used to European goods that they could no longer do without them. To get the goods they had to co-exist with the new conquerors. As the years went on, his divided people were pushed farther and farther into the wilderness while the Europeans pushed their way steadily onward. In the end, the once proud Indians saw most of their hunting ground in the the hands of the white men.

For his time, Pontiac was a remarkable man. He managed to do what no other chief was ever able to do: he inspired many hostile tribes to unite against the common enemy. Even when he was defeated, he did his best to ensure that his people's hunting grounds were kept in native hands. He deserves a high place in the history of North America.

Chapter Five

Joseph Brant

In a park in the centre of the city of Brantford, Ontario, there stands a large statue of Mohawk chief, Joseph Brant, known to his own people as a Thayendaneyeu. He was the most notable Indian of his day, a leader in peace and war and a champion of his people.

Brant was born in the Ohio Valley, south of Lake Ontario in 1742. His family came from the Mohawk Valley in New York, and, according to most people, his father was a chief. For many years, the Mohawks and their friends in the other Iroquois tribes went each year to the Ohio Valley to hunt. Game was scarce in their own country and the vast forests along the Ohio teemed with beavers and other animals. At the end of the winter, most of the hunters returned to their ancestral homes in the beautiful Mohawk Valley. To protect the Ohio hunting grounds from invaders, several young hunters spent years in the valley and some remained there

all their lives.

Joseph was only 8-years-old when his father died. Leaving the Ohio Valley behind, the young widow took Joseph and his older sister Mollie back to their old home. In time, she married a man called Nickolas Brant, from whom Joseph acquired his surname. His Christian name was given to him by the missionaries.

Near Canajoharie Castle, the chief village of the Mohawks, there lived an Indian agent named Colonel William Johnson. It was his job to settle disputes between the Iroquois and the settlers, and to keep the native people on the side of the British. Johnson was a wealthy man who had managed to acquire large tracts of land in the valley. He was very popular with the native people, especially with his nearest neighbors, the Mohawks. He socialized freely with them, learned to speak their language, and joined in their games and dances. Joseph's sister, Mollie, caught Johnson's eye and she lived with him as his wife for the rest of his life.

Young Joseph often visited Johnson's fine stone house near the Colonel's trading post at Fort Johnson. On those visits, he became familiar with English ways and learned a little of the language. Johnson took a special interest in the bright young boy and made plans for his future.

It was at this time that the struggle for the control of North America was coming to a head. Although the French population was only about 75 000 people and the English numbered about 1 500 000, French explorers had penetrated deep into the continent while the English were confined to a narrow strip of land on the Atlantic seaboard.

The first blow was struck in the Ohio Valley. More than fifty years before, the explorer La Salle had discovered the Ohio River and, according to the European laws of the day, the valley belonged to the French. At first, the French paid little attention to the valley; they were more interested in trading and exploring than in farming. Meanwhile, the huge wooded valley continued to be used as Indian hunting grounds. To maintain their control over the region, the Iroquois appointed "half kings" and gave tracts of lands to dependent tribes.

In the 1740s, English settlers began to cross the Allegheny Mountains to make their way into the Ohio, and in 1749, London granted a tract of land to a trading company in the area. Alarmed by this turn of events, the French took action. A row of French forts was built as far south as present-day Pittsburg to put an end to English trading and drive the settlers out of French territory.

When war broke out between the two European powers, the Iroquois were caught in the middle. In their view, the land was theirs. They were justly uneasy about the French posts and wanted to get rid of them. On the other hand, they were unwilling to become embroiled in a war between the two great powers. From past experience, they knew only too well the havoc such a war would wreak. Their lands would be laid waste and their fighting force, already down to a few thousand men, would be reduced still further. Although they were traditionally allies of the English, they did their best to remain neutral.

The early defeats suffered by the British made the Iroquois even more cautious. Eventually, however, William Johnson managed to persuade the Iroquois to fight. Young Joseph took part in the war when he was only about 15-years-old. He later confessed that he hid behind a tree at the sound of the first firing, but recovered his courage and fought bravely from then on.

With the surrender of Montreal in 1760, the war was over and Joseph returned to his homeland. In Lebanon, New Hampshire, there was a boarding school called Moore's

Indian School supported by well-to-do men such as William Johnson. The headmaster, Rev. Eleazer Wheelock, vowed that he could make Christian gentlemen out of "red heathens." Joseph and two other boys from Canajoharie were sent off to Lebanon to be educated.

Joseph Brant (Thayendanegea), Mohawk Chief, 1776? Reprinted, by permission, National Gallery of Canada: 8005.

On their arrival, the three youths were taken to see Reverend Wheelock. "Two of them," he said, "were little better than naked. The other [Joseph Brant] being of a family of distinction was considerably clothed Indian fashion and could speak a few words of English."

To a boy accustomed to open air and freedom, life in a stuffy schoolroom could not have been very pleasant, but Joseph made the best of it. One of his classmates, Samuel Kirkland, who later became a missionary among the Oneidas, describes Joseph as "sprightly, manly, genteel and kindly." Another classmate was Charles Jeffrey Smith, who also intended to work as a missionary. Smith asked Joseph to accompany him as an interpreter. In return for the favor, Smith promised to continue the young man's education. The journey had to be postponed. A letter arrived from home asking the young man to return to Canajohanic. His stepfather was dead and Joseph was the mainstay of his family.

Joseph was scarcely home again before another war broke out. Pontiac, the Ottawa war chief, took up arms against the English at Detroit and vowed to drive the hated enemy out of the west. Before long, the whole western frontier was in a blaze. Seeing their lands taken over by the English, the Senecas split from the other Iroquois tribes and joined the rebels. Sir William Johnson managed to persuade the other Iroquois tribes to remain neutral. Because of his long friendship with the Mohawks, he was able to get them to throw in their lot with the English. In the ensuing war, Brant was in charge of a band of warriors who made raids on the western Indians.

When the fighting ended, Brant returned once more to the Mohawk Valley and built himself a comfortable house with pine floors and bearskin rugs. He was now 23 years of age, old enough to get married. He chose Margaret, the daughter of an Oneida chief. After the usual Mohawk wedding ceremonies, the two young people were married in the Anglican church.

For a few years, Joseph and Margaret lived in peace and quiet while Joseph tilled the land and looked after his livestock. Two children were born, a son named Issac and a daughter, Christine. In 1771, Margaret was struck down with tuberculosis and died.

Taking his little children with him, Brant went to live near the Anglican mission at Fort Hunter where he assisted the minister, Rev. John Stuart, to translate the Bible and the catechism into the Mohawk language. According to Stuart, Brant was "the only person in America equal to such an undertaking." Sir William Johnson also had lots of work for him – translating speeches into native languages and going on peace missions to other tribes. Some people say that it was Johnson who encouraged the Mohawks to have Brant elected war chief.

In 1773, Brant decided to marry Susannah, his deceased wife's sister. Reverend Stuart refused permission because marriage to a sister-in-law was against Anglican law.

However, a Luthern minister did as he was asked and the pair were married. Before the year was out, Susannah too fell victim to the dreaded tuberculosis and Brant was again a widower. Some years later, he was married for the third time to Catherine Croghan, the daughter of Indian agent George Croghan, and they had seven children.

While Joseph lived quietly in the Mohawk Valley, troubles were brewing all around him. By a treaty of 1768, a boundary known as the Stanwix Line was drawn up to separate the English colonies from Indian territory. Although the new agreement gave thousands of acres of Iroquois territory to the settlers, white men were still not satisfied. They poured into Mohawk villages, trying to obtain more land. Even the soldiers sent in to protect the Indians sometimes joined in the land grabbing.

In the early 1770s, the American colonies became more and more dissatisfied with England. As they grew in wealth and power, the settlers resented the taxes imposed upon them. Open clashes took place between settlers and English troops. Sir William Johnson was uneasy. An officer of the British crown, he opposed the rebels. If there was a full scale war, he knew he would need Iroquois help. But could the tribes be depended on to side with the British? With their own love of freedom the Iroquois might be lured to the side of the freedom-loving Americans.

Johnson knew he could depend on his

old friends, the Mohawks who had no love for the settlers. Inch by inch, more settlers were managing to forge their way into Mohawk territory, cheating the Indians left and right. While he was working for Johnson, Joseph Brant saw their trickery at close range. For a few kegs of rum, they managed to obtain large parcels of land. Some of the traders even sold the Mohawks faulty muskets which blew up in their hands.

In the midst of all the turmoil, Johnson died. According to accounts his last words to Brant were, "Joseph, control your people." For Brant, the dying man's words were clear. He would try to get the Iroquois tribes to remain loyal to Britain.

On the death of Sir William Johnson, his son-in-law Guy Johnson took over the position of Indian agent and Brant was appointed his secretary and interpreter. Later the same year, Brant attended a Grand Council of the Iroquois as Johnson's representative. After much discussion, the Iroquois agreed to remain neutral in the war between England and her American colonies.

Harried by the rebel settlers, Guy Johnson decided to go to Montreal for a conference with the Canadian governor, Sir Guy Carleton. The defenceless Mohawks also abandoned their homeland, taking their women and children with them. Carleton praised the Indians for their loyalty, but he was unable to give them land in return for their homeland. Brant knew that without hunting grounds, his people would die of hunger. Since no one in Canada could help him, he decided to cross the Atlantic to England and put his case before the king.

In London, he was received with all the honor due to a great chief. All the important people lined up to meet him and he was received in audience by the King. He stated his people's grievances to the Secretary of State: "We have let the king's subjects have so much of our land for so little value, and they want to cheat us out of the small parts we have left for our women and children." The secretary promised to redress the wrongs as soon as the war was over.

In London, Brant was interviewed by the writer James Boswell and had his portrait painted by the famous artist George Romney. At everyday events Brant was dressed in European clothes, but on state occasions he appeared in his native buckskin with ornaments and feathers. He was invited to dinners and balls and he became the toast of London.

In August 1776, he was back in America. He came ashore secretly somewhere in New York and slipped into Canada without being detected. From then until the end of the war, he fought tirelessly on the British side, for he was convinced that the only way to save his own people was to defeat the American rebels. He distinguished himself at the battle of Long Island. Following that, he and

Captain Gilbert Trice set out in disguise for Iroquois country. Travelling by night and resting by day, the two men reached their destination in safety. At an Iroquois council, he told about his visit to England and his hopes for an English victory. As a result of his efforts, all the Iroquois tribes, except the Oneida and the Tuscarora pledged their support for the British.

One of the bloodiest battles of the war took place at Fort Stanwix, an American fort built on Mohawk land. A British army under General St. Leger and several hundred Indians led by Brant marched on the American fort. In spite of a clever trap, the fort held out. In a ravine nearby, there was fierce hand to hand fighting with heavy losses on both sides. The native people fared the worst in the battle, for they could ill afford the losses they sustained.

For the next two years the war raged on, and Brant's name struck terror into the American settlers. He was adept at short, swift raids and his skill and daring were unsurpassed.

In the chaos of the revolution, the Iroquois league was split. Abandoning their tradition of unity, the nations listened to the advice of the white men and took sides against one another. In the gory struggle, nation was pitted against nation and clan against clan. With the help of the Oneidas, the Americans raided the Mohawk Valley, plundering and looting all before them.

Cattle, wagons, farm implements and farm produce, all fell to the invaders. Brant and his men retaliated by attacking the Oneidas and Tuscaroras and several of the unfortunate people later died of hunger.

For his daring in battle, Brant was given the title of British captain, although, he preferred to fight as a war chief because that rank enabled him to lead more men into battle. By the end of 1780, Brant and his British allies seemed to be gaining the upper hand against the Americans. Their forays had devastated the country from the east coast to the Ohio Valley and far into Pennsylvania. In a letter, the New York governor wrote that his state was on the verge of ruin.

The tide turned when a French fleet moved into Chesapeake Bay to come to the aid of the Americans. The British forces who had entrenched themselves at Yorktown, Virginia were beseiged and forced to surrender. A few further skirmishes brought the war to an end.

Brant's last service in the war was at Fort Oswego, New York. In June 1782, he arrived at Oswego with 300 men to protect the fort, only to find no food, no moccasins and no ammunition for his men. Disappointed though he was, he went to work with a will. "I never saw men work so hard and it greatly encourages the troops," reported the English commander, Major Ross. After leaving the fort to harry the Americans, word reached Brant that the war was over.

In the peace treaty, the native people were forgotten. Part of the land ceded to the Americans was former Indian hunting grounds. The unfortunate native allies who had fought so gallantly for Britain and who had suffered hardship and starvation could not believe their ears.

On behalf of his people, Brant approached the English commander, Sir Frederick Haldimand, at Montreal. Haldimand heard him out. Then he offered the Iroquois a tract of land north of Lake Ontario near the Bay of Quinte. The Senecas were worried at the news. Their home was in the Genesee Valley close to the American settlers and they begged Brant to settle near them and help to protect them.

Brant felt sorry for the Senecas. He went back to Haldimand and this time he was given a grant of land closer to the Seneca, on the Grand River between Lake Huron and Lake Erie. This was to be the new home of the Mohawks and any other Iroquois tribes who wished to move there. Through Grant's efforts, the destitute people received some money to help get them started in their new homeland.

Now reduced to 400 souls, the Mohawks settled down on the lands surrounding present-day Brantford. With some of the money from Haldimand, Brant supervised the construction of a sawmill. He wanted his people to live in comfortable wooden houses like those of the white settlers. On a small hillock beside a bridge spanning the Grand River he built a home for himself and his family. He bought livestock and farm utensils for his people and tried to encourage them to farm the land. Knowing the value of education, he had a schoolhouse constructed and he received an allowance of $25 a year for a teacher. Soon his people had a council house for their meetings and an Anglican church for the Christian natives.

Shortly afterwards, Brant's old friend, Rev. James Stuart, came to visit the Mohawks in their new home. By then, there were about 700 people in the village. Reverend Stuart conducted a service in the newly erected church. "The pulpit was trimmed with crimson," he wrote, "and the Ten Commandments in the old Mohawk language were on the wall behind it." The people pressed Reverend Stuart to stay among them, but he had orders to return to America.

While Brant was looking after the welfare of his own people in the Grand River Valley, he had not forgotten the other native people who were in danger of losing their land. Knowing that strength came from unity, he held a number of small council meetings to try to bring the tribes together. Finally, a large meeting of Iroquois and western Indians was held at Sandusky. At the meeting Brant explained why the Mohawks had fought on the British side during the war. He concluded his speech with a plea for unity: "Our interests are all alike. Nor should anything be done but by the voice of the whole."

Governor Haldimand sent an account of the meeting to England: "The Indians understand the nature and obligations of treaties as well as the most civilized nations. They know that nothing can be binding without their consent. Their general confederacy is to defend their country against invaders."

In 1785, Brant made his second voyage to England to plead for his people. One matter was uppermost in his mind. He wanted to be sure that the land on the Grand River truly belonged to his people to do with as they wished. It was not enough to have the use of the property. If his people truly owned the land, they could sell small portions to help them get on their feet after all the losses they had sustained in the war. The forests were without game, so no money could be made from fur-trading and some of the native people knew little about agriculture. Even if they did, they would first have to clear the forest. Brant also asked the Secretary for help in the event that the Indian people would be forced to take up arms to defend their homelands from the Americans. His request was justified. After all, his own warriors had come to the aid of the British in their hour of need, and he was lame from the wounds he had received in the war with America.

Brant put the case before Lord Sydney, the British Secretary of War. The Indians were destitute, he told him. He asked for immediate payments to help his people "to stock their farms and get such articles and materials as all settlements in new countries require and which is out of their power before they are paid for their losses."

While Sydney was thinking the matter over, Brant was again presented at court. The great nobles and statesmen of the day lined up to entertain him. One noble lady wrote: "I dined with the famous Indian chief, Captain Brant, at the General's. His manners are polished. In his dress, he showed off to advantage the half-military and half-savage costume. His countenance was manly and intelligent, and his disposition mild."

Once, Brant attended a fancy dress ball in London in his native costume. A guest reached out his hand to touch the chief's face, thinking it was a mask. For fun Brant gave a blood-curdling scream, scaring some of the guests half to death.

Three months went by before Lord Sydney was ready to reply to Brant's requests. His decision was that the native people would receive compensation for their war losses and Brant himself would get a pension for his service to the crown. Sydney made it clear that he approved of Brant's plan to bring all the tribes together so long as the native people kept the peace. He concluded by expressing his love and concern for "England's Indian children" and he promised to look after their welfare in the future.

In reality, the British government had no intention of taking up the Indian cause. England was in a depression and the last thing she needed was any trouble with her former colonies in America. What the country wanted was trade, and America was a likely customer. If the native people should take up arms to defend their lands, they could expect no help from England.

After his visit to England, Brant was more convinced than ever that the Indian people should unite. Left to themselves, without any bargaining power, individual bands were selling land to American settlers for little or nothing. At a General Council in Detroit, Brant implored the assembled tribes to work together. An address was sent to the United States government advising them that the Congress must treat with the Indian Confederation as a whole, not with individuals.

All his efforts came to nothing. Lured by the white man's goods, Indians continued to barter their land away. As waves of settlers swept into Indian lands, skirmishes broke out on the border. The situation worsened and General St. Clair was sent to the Ohio Valley to quell the revolt. Brant was ill at the time and took no part in the fighting, but he did send some of his men to the aid of the warring tribe. The assembled natives pounced on St. Clair's army and cut it to pieces.

The United States Congress was alarmed. The last thing President George Washington wanted was another costly struggle along the new nation's borders. Plans were stepped up to call a meeting with native leaders and settle the land disputes once and for all.

Negotiations proceeded at a snail's pace. To try to break the deadlock, the Americans sent a letter to Brant inviting him to Philadelphia to discuss Indian welfare in general. Brant considered the proposal carefully before coming to a decision. He decided to go, on condition that he would be regarded as a spokesman for the other Indians and that he would have a face-to-face meeting with Washington himself. The Americans accepted his terms.

Meanwhile, the British were none too happy. What if Brant turned his back on his old allies and became friendly with the United States government? Governor George Simcoe and other British officers warned him against going to Philadelphia, but their warnings fell on deaf ears. Conscious of his negotiating skills, Brant hoped to make a good settlement with the war-weary Americans.

In the spring of 1792, Brant set out on horseback for Philadelphia. On his way, he passed through his old homeland in the

Mohawk Valley, now in the hands of American settlers. After a short stay in the city of New York to visit old friends, he pressed on to Philadelphia.

Washington did his best to win Brant's support. He swore up and down that the Americans had no desire to take any Indian land north of the Muskegum River. If Brant would only persuade the western Indians to agree to that boundary line, he would receive a large sum of money and an annual pension. Brant was offended at being offered what he considered a bribe. He refused the money, but agreed to use his influence with the western Indians.

On his way home, Brant fell sick of a fever and was confined to bed in Niagara for some time. When he finally arrived at the Indian meeting place, he found that the chiefs had already held a meeting and rejected the President's proposal. Brant called another meeting the following year. After long and heated debate, the western Indians again refused to accept the new boundary line.

Brant was disappointed. In his final address he said: "You are come to a final resolution. We hope success will attend you. It is not in our power to assist you. We must first remove our people from among the Americans. If any choose to remain, they must abide the consequences." Then he left the meeting.

More blood was spilled before the western Indians were forced to surrender to the Americans. At long last, the settlement known as the Jay Treaty was signed in 1796. By its terms the British withdrew their soldiers from the western forts, the Indians laid down their arms and the Americans took control of the Ohio Valley.

Portrait of Etow oh Koam, Mohawk Chief.
Reprinted, by permission
National Archives of Canada: 0082

Brant's heart was saddened by the plight of the native people. Deprived of their lands, worn out by fighting in the white man's wars, the once proud people had been brought to their knees. On his own reserve on the Grand River, the situation was better. Although the people still had not received clear title to their land, they had snug wooden cabins with a few sticks of furniture surrounded by gardens with corn and other vegetables.

Brant's declining years were peaceful enough, except for one terrible tragedy. His son, Isaac, had always been a troublesome youth. The older he got, the worse he became. In his drunken bouts, he became quarrelsome and violent. One day he was quarrelling in a tavern and his father went in to quieten him. There was a struggle between father and son, and Joseph accidentally stabbed Isaac in the hand. The young man refused to have the wound attended to, it became infected and he died.

At a council meeting, the chiefs exonerated Brant of all blame and the Canadian authorities did the same. Nevertheless, the death of his first-born son in such an unnatural way was a burden to Brant for the rest of his life. It is said that he kept the fatal knife in his room and often wept when he looked at it.

Other incidents plagued him as well. He never stopped pressing the government to give his people clear title to their land to dispose of as they saw fit. Governor Simcoe strongly opposed Brant's proposals. The truth was that Simcoe thought Brant had too much power with his people and should be kept in his place. In one of his letters to England, the Governor remarked: "He [Brant] is not so respectful and proper as he ought to be."

Finally, Brant took his case to the British Ambassador in Philadelphia. He even hinted that he might consider joining with the French who were said to be considering an uprising against the English. Certain people in the Department of Indian Affairs began to accuse Brant of dishonesty. A disgruntled group of Indians held a council meeting at Buffalo Creek, New York and called on him to resign. When the Grand Council of the Six Nations heard of the meeting, they treated the subject with contempt: "It is not reasonable, that we should be dictated to by such a council held at such a distance and with such members."

At a General Council meeting, Brant arose to his feet and produced all his financial records. William Claus, the leader of the rebel group was soundly rebuked for the false charges and Brant's records were approved. It was later discovered that Claus himself had embezzled a lot of Indian money.

In a last ditch attempt to settle the question of land ownership, Brant set out again for England. On his way to New York to catch the boat, he suffered a heart attack and was forced to return home. He lingered for six months. Then in late November, 1807, he died. With his dying breath, he spoke of his concern for his people. Turning to John Norton, an old friend and adopted chief, he said, "Have pity on the poor Indians. If you can get any influence with the great, endeavor to do them all the good you can." He was buried beside the walls of the church he had helped to build.

Joseph Brant was a forward-looking man. He adopted several of the white man's innovations and he knew the value of education. But he could be critical of English society. He deplored the differences between the rich and the poor and he was appalled at the custom of throwing people into prison for debt. In all his dealings, he never forgot that he was an Indian. Brant took pride in his roots and he did his best to help his people keep their dignity and independence.

Chapter Six

Crowfoot

Chief Crowfoot, diplomat and peace-maker was the heroic protector of the welfare of his nation, the doomed Blackfoot Confederacy. The nation comprised three main tribes speaking the same language: the Peigan, the Blood and the Blackfoot, sometimes call the Northern Blackfoot. The people of this rich and powerful nation, were buffalo hunters and roamed over a large territory stretching from what is now central Alberta, deep into the centre of the continent. For thousands of years the buffalo roamed over the prairies in massive, dark rolling waves and they provided almost total sustenance for the Blackfeet.

Crowfoot was born into the Blood tribe, the son of Packs-a-Knife and his wife, Attacked-Toward-Home, while they were camped near the Belly River in southern Alberta. He was given the name Astohkomi, meaning Shot-Close which was used until he reached manhood when another name

suitable to his character and conduct was chosen.

Camp was moved frequently and Attacked-Toward-Home would pack their belongings into a bundle which could be carried on the travois, two poles tied tightly together at one end and placed over the neck of the horse, with the untied ends dragging on the ground. Skins, blankets and bundles were fastened to the poles and the children were securely placed on the bundles. When the tribe camped, the poles could be used for the teepee.

When the prairie blossomed with the crocuses, wild roses and shooting stars, the warriors went to hunt for the buffalo. These magnificent animals were still plentiful when Crowfoot was young, even though the white man was making his way west. In the times long ago, before the coming of the horse, the braves hunted the beasts on foot with bows and arrows. The chase was exhilarating and the men became very skilled in shooting from their fast ponies which they prized. Even with the introduction of firearms most continued to use the bow and arrow because it was difficult to reload a gun on a fast horse, and each hunter's distinctive arrows identified the beasts he had shot and could claim.

BULL-BOAT

Bull-boat

Sometimes the tribe would use a jumping pound to kill the buffalo. Scouts guided the herds to a cliff and drove the weak sighted animals over the brink while those below on the plain waited to slaughter them. The women of the tribe helped to butcher the meat and prepared a great feast in the camp. Some of the meat would be cut in strips and smoked over a slow fire. The hides, horns and bones were all used for tools, clothes and warm cover for the winter. After a short time, the tribe would be on the

move again and the women gathered up the dried and smoked meat into a bundle to be placed on the travois.

The hunters also occupied themselves in raiding enemy camps for horses, and often the Bloods and other tribes were at war. One year, Shot-Close's father joined the warriors to raid the Crows far to the south to get horses. He did not return from the expedition and Attacked-Toward-Home mourned him, cutting her hair and singing mourning songs outside the camp. Then she moved back into her father's lodge and the old man took over the education of the young boys, teaching them the stories and skills of their tribe.

One summer a group of Blackfoot warriors, returning from a raid came to the Blood camp on the Belly River. One of the warriors, Many-Names, was attracted to the young widow, Attacked-Toward-Home, and she agreed to be his wife and live with his people, the Blackfeet to the north. Her father was distressed at the thought of losing the boys so it was arranged for Shot-Close to stay his grandfather. However, the boy was determined to be with his mother and brother, and he followed them on foot far out on the prairie. At last the whole group turned back and sought out the grandfather's teepee. To settle the dilemma, the old man left his lodge and travelled with them north to the Bow River, to the Blackfoot Crossing.

As Shot-Close settled down with the Blackfeet, he was given a new name, Bear-Ghost; but all his life his mother called him by his first name, Shot-Close. With the other boys he learned to ride horses and took part in bare back races. Each young boy formed a partnership with a friend of his own age, and Bear-Ghost's comrade was Wolf-Orphan. They played together, guarded the horses, helped to break the young colts and looked out for each other. When the time came, they would go out on warlike expeditions together. At the annual Sun Dance ceremonies, the boys admired the young men who underwent the trials which would prove them to be brave warriors. Some chose to be dragged along the ground tied to a horse. Others danced around the sacred Sun Dance pole to which they were attached by thongs threaded through the muscles of their chest. They danced until exhausted or until the thongs tore the muscles.

In his early teens, Bear-Ghost was allowed to accompany the warriors when they left the camp to raid a hostile tribe. As a result of his bravery and cunning on these expeditions, he was allowed to take a new name and he chose the name of his dead father, Packs-A-Knife. The natives believed that names were a possession of the family and the tribe and could be passed on if the person was worthy. However, the young man's outstanding behaviour in another important raid earned him a new name. A war party was organized against the Blackfeet's long time enemies, the Crows. The Blackfoot warriors travelled south through Montana and when their scouts' found the location of the large Crow encampment, they saw a decorated teepee which had been stolen from the Blackfeet. The leader of the party, a Blood chief, said that whoever reached the teepee first and struck it would be a future leader of his people. The young Packs-A-Knife was determined to get to the teepee and though wounded in the arm managed to reach the decorated lodge and struck it with his whip. This exploit earned him the right to a new name and he chose the name of a former great chief of his nation, Crowfoot, the name by which he is best known.

Now a proven warrior, Crowfoot went on many more raids. On one of these he was struck with a bullet in the back and had to be carried back to the Blackfoot camp where he was treated by the medicine man. Although he recovered, the bullet remained lodged in his back and troubled him the rest of his life.

Most of the Blackfoot assaults were on the Crees to the north of the Blackfoot territory. On one such raid, Crowfoot daringly pursued a Cree warrior on foot, risking ambush in the thick brush. He seized the Cree by his long hair, plunged his knife into the Cree's chest and scalped him. For the rest of his life, Crowfoot kept that knife ornamented with feathers. In the camp, he acted with other warriors as a member of one of the military societies, the All Brave Dogs. They were often assigned tasks by the chief and councillors and sometimes they were required to act as a sort of police force to keep order during the hunt.

Crowfoot
Reprinted, by permission,
Glenbow Archives

Crowfoot was tall, slim, dignified and reserved, and his courage and intelligent leadership were evident. His chief, Three

Suns, admired the young warrior and gave him an owl's head which Crowfoot wore always on the crown of his head in his long hair. Three Suns believed that the talisman would protect the young warrior and help him become a leader of his people. Crowfoot by this time was rich with many horses, and he had married a Blackfoot girl, Cutting-Woman. Though he took more wives into his lodge, she remained his favorite, sitting beside him in the teepee and accompanying him on some of his visits. For a man to have several wives was a sign of his wealth and Crowfoot usually had four at one time for there was much work to do. Also with him in his lodge was his mother and his children; and close by in his other lodges were his relatives and the young warriors who helped him with his horses.

Three Suns shared the leadership of the Northern Blackfeet with two other chieftians, Old Sun and Old Swan. These men were wise and peaceful, and maintained good relations with the Hudson's Bay traders at Fort Edmonton and Rocky Mountain House. When Old Swan died, his nephew, Big Swan, succeeded him but he was warlike and hated the whites. Even some of his own tribe disapproved of him and chose to join Three Suns' group. In time, Three Suns was succeeded by his son who was also called Three Suns. He too was peaceful man but did not have the leadership qualities of his father and many of the tribe looked to Crowfoot for leadership. Those who were dissatisfied moved their teepees to Crowfoot's camp. The new tribe took the name Big Pipes, but over the course of time they were called the Moccasin Band. Crowfoot acted like a father to his people, making sure they all had enough to eat and sending presents to the old and infirm. The young unmarried braves helped in the administration of the tribe and Crowfoot's wives cooked for them. When the band moved, Crowfoot made sure that everyone had a means of transportation.

In the winter, the Blackfeet camped in the parkland, north of the Red Deer River where in the bush they could find shelter from the snow. Three Suns and his group camped a few miles from the Moccasins. While the Blackfeet were there, Father Lacombe, the pioneer missionary, visited them. He had been working with the Crees and the Métis around Fort Edmonton and St. Albert, and decided to try to convert the Blackfeet, but they were a proud people and chose not to change their religion or way of life. Father Lacombe could see that the natives would have to give up their hunting economy in favor of agriculture because the buffalo were rapidly disappearing. Working at St. Albert, he had tried to cultivate the land and in the summer he travelled with the natives bringing with him his plough, potatoes and some grain. Though he showed them by example how to cultivate and plant,

he found that he was able to teach only the women. It was the traditional task of the women to gather and preserve food while the men hunted.

In the late autumn, he travelled south to Crowfoot's camp on the Battle River where he was welcomed, though his knowledge of the language was poor. With him, as always he carried his identifying flag with its red cross on a white background. After spending a short time with the Moccasins, Father Lacombe moved to the camp of Three Suns. In the middle of a cold, snowy night, the Crees attacked. In the camp were only eighty Blackfoot warriors to face hundreds of Crees. They fought valiantly but the enemy pushed into the camp, scalping victims, shrieking and firing their muskets into the teepees. Father Lacombe rushed from Three Suns' lodge where he had been asleep and when dawn came, with some hope of stopping the slaughter, he rushed out before the Cree warriors, waving his banner and shouting to them in their own language. The Crees could not see him in the dim light and the noise was too great for them to hear. The sound of battle roused Crowfoot's camp and he, leading his warriors, hastened to join the fray. With this powerful reinforcement, the Blackfeet went on the attack and drove the Crees off. The camp was in a pitiful state, for many of the lodges were torn and ruined, pemmican and horses taken and many people wounded. Three Suns' leg was shattered by an enemy bullet but Crowfoot was unhurt although he had fought fiercely at the head of his warriors.

As more whites moved into the area, many of the Blackfeet were very distrustful of them and were encouraged in their war-like mood by such chiefs as Big Swan. In 1866, the chief of the Bloods sent a message to Fort Edmonton asking that a trading party be sent to meet the Blackfeet. John Cunningham, an employee of the Hudson's Bay Company lead the party of loaded wagons into the Blackfoot encampment and began to unpack the trade goods. Irritated by the fact that the drivers were Métis and friendly with the Crees, the mood of some of the Blackfeet became threatening. Big Swan, who hated the whites, tried to stir his warriors to violence with boastful speeches. When he insulted Cunningham by throwing a tattered old buffalo robe at the trader's feet, Cunningham knew that the situation was dangerous. He ordered the wagons to be reloaded. Suddenly, Crowfoot stepped forward to stand between the trading party and Big Swan's warriors. Defying the angry braves, he provided a safe escort for the traders back to Edmonton and prevented a slaughter of the Métis.

Cunningham was greatly impressed by Chief Crowfoot as was Richard Hardisty, the Hudson Bay Company trader at Rocky Mountain House, who considered him his friend. These men recognized Crowfoot's

great leadership qualities and intelligence, and treated him as head chief. When the Blackfeet went to trade at Rocky Mountain House, the chiefs entered the stockade while their tribesmen camped outside. Crowfoot, leader of the All Brave Dogs was honored when he was asked if some of them would act as guards for the large encampment. Crowfoot was presented with a British flag, a chief's uniform of scarlet cloth and a tall black hat decorated with an eagle plume, and he in turn presented the trader with one of his best horses.

In 1869, the Blackfeet suffered greatly from the small pox. Because of this they were not welcome at the trading posts and other tribes shunned them. The power of the Blackfoot nation was declining. Formerly they had been known as the fiercest and most numerous nation on the northwestern plains. Now the disappearance of the buffalo, the white man's diseases and his religion were all weakening their ancient vigorous and free life. When Three Suns died from small pox, Crowfoot became head chief of the tribe. He seldom went out on a war party and often he prevented his young warriors from doing so. He was quick tempered and was stern but just in his government of the tribe.

In time, a peace treaty was signed with the Crees and they visited in one another's camp. One night, the mother of Crowfoot's dead son, who had been killed in an earlier raid, told the chief that she had seen a young Cree warrior named Poundmaker who looked very like her son. Crowfoot too was struck by the resemblance. As all the young man's family were dead and he had no close relatives, the young warrior agreed to join the Blackfeet and become Crowfoot's adopted son. Though the peace treaty with the Crees did not last long, Poundmaker stayed with his adopted father. Later, when he did leave, Crowfoot gave him horses and other presents.

The next plague that faced the Blackfoot nation was alcohol. The Hudson's Bay Company had not allowed it in the territory they controlled; but when the territory was transferred from the Company to the Canadian government, there were no rules in place and the wily whiskey traders from the United states immediately moved into Canadian territory to rob the natives of their furs.

At the notorious Fort Whoop-up, the Long Knives, as the Blackfeet called the Americans, traded whiskey and rifles for buffalo hides. Crowfoot drank in moderation but many of the natives could not resist the new, potent drink and gave all they possessed for it. Their clothes and teepees went unrepaired and their children hungry. The young men got into drunken fights and Crowfoot could no longer restrain them. He could see they were in danger from the Crees who had not come in contact with the Long Knives and who saw the growing weakness of their enemies, the Blackfeet. In fact, the Crees were planning to attack them and take over their hunting grounds. The situation became so desperate that the federal government, realizing that they had to take steps to control the situation, formed the North West Mounted Police to keep law and order in the west. The message about this move was brought to Crowfoot by the Protestant missionary, Rev. John McDougall. Crowfoot greeted the news with gratitude for it meant that the Long Knives would be driven out and equal justice for white and native would be assured.

The Mounted Police built a fort on the Old Man River and Crowfoot sent his foster brother, Three Bulls, to report to Colonel Macleod that American traders were operating what was now an illegal post. Macleod acted immediately and confiscated the whiskey, the buffalo robes, the guns and the horses and punished the men. This prompt action greatly impressed Crowfoot and his people. Colonel Macleod sent his interpreter, Jerry Potts, requesting a meeting with the chiefs of the Blackfoot nation. At the grand council, Macleod explained how the Queen had sent her soldiers to restore order to the country. Crowfoot, using his skills as an orator, thanked the Queen for sending the Police to save his people. He and Macleod took to each other and remained friends.

With the whiskey trade halted,

Crowfoot tried to guide his people so that they could adapt to new conditions for he realized the whites were in indian lands to stay. If his warriors stole the horses of another tribe, he made them return them. Gradually the Blackfeet regained some of their old property and prestige. Though Colonel Macleod had said the Police had not come to take land from the natives, inevitably the settlers began moving across the plains into the hunting grounds. Crowfoot could see great misfortune for his people and consulted Rev. John McDougall. The missionary tried to explain to the chief the arrangements and treaties which had been made by the government with other native tribes in Canada. Crowfoot then called a meeting of the Blackfoot nation and they drew up a petition to the Lieutenant Governor asking that representatives be sent to meet the Blackfeet.

Before the commissioners could arrive to deal with the request, Crowfoot received a message from Sitting Bull, great chief of the fierce Sioux in the United States. Sitting Bull said that he had gathered a large force of warriors ready to attack the army of the United States and he wanted the Blackfeet to join them in the struggle to save their lands and their way of life. After consulting his allies, the Bloods and the Peigans, Crowfoot found that they were unwilling to join Sitting Bull and a message to that effect was sent to the Sioux. Sitting Bull replied with

the threat that when the Sioux had won their battles with the whites in the United States, they would come north and drive out the North West Mounted Police and all the white settlers and destroy the Blackfoot nation. At that point, Crowfoot consulted with Inspector Cecil Denny who was friendly with the natives and sensitive to their problems. He assured Crowfoot that his people would be protected by the forces of the Canadian government. Crowfoot then made an impressive speech affirming his loyalty to the Queen and expressing his hopes that in the face of the incursions of the whites and Métis from the north that the Blackfeet would be helped and not forced to starve. When Inspector Denny sent his report of Crowfoot's speech to Ottawa, the officials were so impressed that they sent a copy to the Queen.

Sitting Bull did defeat the forces of the United States government sent against him and then moved north to escape retribution. He settled in the safety of the Milk River area but this put more pressure on the scarce herds of buffalo. When Crowfoot and his tribe wandered south, they camped near the Sioux and Sitting Bull sent another message to Crowfoot with a gift of tobacco and saying that he wanted peace. The two great chiefs met and were impressed with one another. The tribes celebrated with a friendship dance and Sitting Bull said he would name his son after his new friend.

The authorities were now anxious to sign a treaty with the Blackfeet in order to keep them from being tempted to join with the Sioux. The Crees to the north had already signed Treaty 6 in 1876, by which they gave up most of their land. The Indian nations had no concept of owning land and it was difficult for them to understand what they were giving up. The authorities now called the Blackfoot tribes together. They met at Blackfoot Crossing on the Bow River, and celebrated the occasion with drumming and dancing. Some took the rations handed out by the commissioners, but Crowfoot was too proud to do so before the proposed treaty was signed. Old Sun announced that he was too old to decide for his people and suggested that Crowfoot decide for them. It was a great responsibility and Crowfoot knew how vulnerable his people were. With Treaty 7, the Blackfeet gave up thousands of miles of grassland on which their people had hunted for centuries. It was a tragic moment and Crowfoot made a moving speech in which he asked that the Mounted Police protect the interests of his people and act toward them in a charitable way. The next day, after the signing, he made an even more moving speech asking that the whites protect the hills, forests, valleys, waters and wild life which shared the land with man, all the abundance which his people had enjoyed for centuries. Unlike the whites who regarded nature as theirs to exploit, the wise natives knew that man and nature must live in harmony.

On the Sunday after the signing, the Blackfeet gave an exhibition of a sham battle which in reality was half in earnest for many of the Blackfeet distrusted the treaty. Some of them knew what had happened in the United States where the government had not honored the provisions of the treaties signed there. The warriors, stripped to their loin clothes, wearing their feathered headresses and painted for war, circled the camp uttering wild cries. The whites were very apprehensive, although they remained outwardly calm.

Before they left the Blackfoot Crossing, the authorities wanted to negotiate with the Blackfeet about the reserved land for the tribes. The idea of being confined to a limited area was utterly foreign to these nomads of the prairies and again Crowfoot did not really understand what he was signing. At this time, he chose a reserve which would accommodate the whole Blackfoot nation so that they could stay together and be strengthened in their negotiations with the whites. However, the authorities and Colonel Macleod decided that it would be safer for the whites if the Bloods were separated from the other Blackfeet. When Inspector Denny was sent to convey this news to Crowfoot, the chief became so angry that Colonel Macleod himself had to visit the camp where he persuaded the Chief to accept the decision.

The winter of 1878-79 was dreadful for Crowfoot's people. Formerly, the administration had supplied them with buffalo meat, but now there was such a scarcity that the government had to buy beef from a dealer who drove cattle from the south and charged high prices for the produce. The authorities underestimated the need for meat and Inspector Denny at Fort Calgary was soon faced with the problem of starving Blackfeet, reduced to eating their dogs and boiling their moccasins. Inspector Denny on his own authority supplied them with more food. Thereafter, they trusted him as a friend. More supplies came in the summer with the newly appointed Indian commissioner Edgar Dewdney, but the flour, tea and beef were all gone by the autumn. The commissioner's solution to the problem was to tell Crowfoot and his people to move south over the border where he said the buffalo were still plentiful. But the move to Montana meant that the whiskey traders entered the camp and the dreadful days of violence and drunkeness began again.

While they were in Montana, Crowfoot met the Métis leader, Louis Riel. Exiled from Canada because of his former rebellion, he was travelling with a Métis hunting party which arrived at the Blackfoot encampment. Riel welcomed the opportunity to talk with Crowfoot and tell him of his plans to unite the Métis with the Crees, the Sioux and the Blackfeet to crush the white settlers and set up their own government. Riel warned Crowfoot and his people that the Canadian government was not to be trusted. Some of the native leaders were swayed by Riel's persuasive arguments. But Crowfoot knew that his people could never win against the forces of change and the governments of the United States and Canada, however just the native grievances. Moreover, he continued to put his trust in his friends, the Mounted Police.

Crowfoot wanted to take his people back to Canada but Dewdney discouraged him because of the expense of feeding them, so the Blackfeet set up camp for the winter at Fort Carrol. The Crees under Big Bear and the Métis with their leader, Louis Riel, also wintered there. The three men often conferred and Riel's followers tried to stir up rebellion in the camps, but Crowfoot was not persuaded. All winter the whiskey traders moved through the camps, horses were stolen and the young warriors unable to go on the hunt, often became so violent that Crowfoot could not control them. As spring approached Crowfoot told his band to break up into small groups so that they would have more chance of finding the buffalo. Some of the little groups slowly wandered back to Fort Macleod where they waited for their chief. Crowfoot had remained in the United States hoping to find enough meat for winter but his stay was cut short when his warriors raided the Crows and took their horses and supplies. Crowfoot knew that if this booty was not returned, the United States Army would be after them. So the Blackfeet started for Canada with few horses, little supplies and hardly any in furs. Most of the group had to walk and for lack of horses abandoned their belongings. It was a sad group that straggled into Fort Macleod to join the rest of their tribe. The Blackfeet were being fed with rations supplied by the government through Indian agents some of whom were ignorant and rough and insulted the proud natives. Moreover, the meat and flour supplied by merchants who were cheating the government were often of poor quality.

When the Blackfeet settled again near Blackfoot Crossing, they found that the Crees had moved south and were camped only a few miles away. A dispute broke out and a Cree was killed. Denny went to investigate and persuaded the two groups to meet and negotiate. The Crees only agreed to this because they knew they were in the wrong moving into Blackfoot territory. A large teepee in which discussion could take place was set up between the camps. When Denny arrived, Chief Crowfoot threw down a beautifully dressed buffalo robe as a present. As the other chiefs arrived, they too brought buffalo robes which Denny could not refuse for fear of giving offense to the chiefs. Thus behind him, as he sat, was a high pile of beautiful robes. As it turned out, the Police were very grateful for them in the cold of the ensuing winter. With Denny was a captain from the United States who was astonished that the small company of Mounted Police could bring peace so easily and quickly between the tribes, surrounded as the whites were by thousands of natives.

In 1881, the news came to the Blackfeet that the Queen's son-in-law, the Marquis of Lorne, Governor General of Canada, would be travelling through the West. He came to the camp with Poundmaker, now a chief of the Crees who was acting as guide to the royal party. Crowfoot was overjoyed to see his son, tall, handsome and a leader of his people. When Chief Crowfoot stood before the royal visitor in tattered clothing and showing signs of the suffering he and his tribe had endured, he pleaded for help for his starving people. The Marquis could only advise Crowfoot to guide his people to till the land on the reserve, a drastic transition from the free exciting days of the buffalo hunt. Poundmaker stayed in the camp for a few days giving great pleasure to his old friend who regarded him as a son. Crowfoot had lost many of his own children to tuberculosis.

Due to the arrogance and incompetence of government officials, discontent and rebellion was rife in the tribe. When in one dispute a Blackfoot carrying a gun had threatened a dishonest trader and was unjustly arrested, Crowfoot angrily protested. Colonel Macleod, now a magistrate, knew that injustice had been done but felt he had to punish the native for having a firearm. From that day forward, Crowfoot never again completely trusted any white men. Inspector Denny tried to remedy the situation in the camp by sending more understanding and sympathetic agents to the reserve.

The discontent of the natives was heightened by the building of the railroad. Inspector Denny tried to reassure Crowfoot and his councillors that the "Iron Horse" would bring food more quickly to the natives. However, when the surveyors started their work they chose the right of way to go along the edge of the Blackfoot reserve and a portion of it would actually go through the Blackfoot land. When the natives saw the workmen, they attempted to stop them and fearing dangerous violence, Father Lacombe intervened and visited the reserve with presents of flour, sugar, tea and tobacco. He assured the people that Dewdney would come and right matters. A few days later, the Lieutenant Governor did arrive and promised the Blackfeet new land to replace what they would lose, and if that did not satisfy them, then the right of way would be moved. With the cooperation of Crowfoot, the matter was settled but when the trains began to run, the smoke, the noise and the sparks from the engine so troubled

the camp that the warriors were ready to tear up the tracks with a word from their chief.

The change to life on the reserve was not an easy one. Crowfoot refused to live in the house built on the reserve and remained in his teepee, but he did plant a field of turnips and potatoes as an example to his people. Though he had lost much of his power to influence events, he acted as a wise mediator among the Blackfeet. He also kept in touch with Big Bear and his other friends in the different tribes. Riel, too, sent messengers to him, for the Métis leader was now back in Canada, rallying his forces for another rebellion. When the Mounted Police sent men into Crowfoot's lodge to arrest Riel's messenger, Crowfoot was outraged for the man had not broken any law. The chief insisted on being at the messenger trial to see that justice was done. The incident shook Crowfoot's trust in the Mounted Police. The Lieutenant Governor, Dewdney, was very worried about this blunder and asked Crowfoot and the other chiefs of the Blackfeet to travel on the railroad to Regina and Winnipeg to meet him. On this journey, the Blackfeet saw for the first time the impressive strength of the whites in their cities, now so close to their ancient lands. He and the others realized that they could not win against these forces and that they must cooperate while seeking more justice for their people.

The Riel rebellion broke out in 1885

when the government of Sir John A. Mac-Donald refused to pay attention to the legitimate claims of the Métis to have their rights to their farm lands confirmed and their requests for schools and hospitals granted. Though Crowfoot and his fellow chiefs refused to rise in rebellion, they sympathised profoundly with the Crees and the Métis and sheltered any of them who came to their camps. Alarmed at all the unrest, Dewdney appointed Denny his personal representative in the area for he knew the Blackfeet trusted him as much as any white man. When the rebellious Crees sent a message to Crowfoot to tell him that if the Blackfeet did not join them, the Crees would launch an attack against them, Crowfoot consulted Denny. The Inspector met with the chief and told him that his people would always be protected against the Crees. Crowfoot then sent another message of loyalty to the Queen which was received with great relief by the troubled government. Though some of his own warriors and natives from other tribes accused Crowfoot of disloyalty to his people, in reality his only interest was in protecting the Blackfeet and he showed great courage and wisdom in his firm stand for peace.

Though he was a chief of the Crees, Poundmaker, too, tried to prevent bloodshed. In spite of his efforts, Poundmaker's camp had been attacked by the whites during the Riel rebellion. He and Big Bear were imprisoned though they had done their best to restrain their followers and protect the settlers. Crowfoot sent a petition to Lieutenant Governor Dewdney on Poundmaker's behalf and the latter succeeded in getting the young man freed after serving only a few months of his sentence. But even those few months in captivity had broken him and he travelled to Crowfoot's camp only to die at the Sun Dance ceremonies on the banks of the Bow River. He was mourned by the chief as a son.

Crowfoot was still suffering from his loss when he was visited by the "Great Chieftain", Sir John A. MacDonald who was travelling across Canada on the railroad. As a result of the meeting, Crowfoot received an invitation to visit the Prime Minister in addition to taking part in ceremonies to unveil a monument to Joseph Brant, the great Mohawk chief. Crowfoot, accompanied by Father Lacombe, an interpreter and his half brother, Three Bulls, left ahead of the rest of the party so that they could visit Montreal and Quebec City. All who met him were struck by his dignified appearance and everywhere he was treated as an honored visitor. Crowfoot was impressed with the sights of the cities, the great river St. Lawrence and the fortifications at Quebec city. Their next stop was Ottawa where they were joined by the other Blackfoot chiefs and they were all presented to the Prime Minister. Crowfoot spoke with his customary dignity and asked that since the buffalo had gone, large farms be given to his people so that they could feed themselves. Gifts of money on this occasion, as well as assurance of good will were given to them. Crowfoot by this time was worn out by the journey and felt that he could not go to Brantford for the ceremony. The other chiefs left and Crowfoot, Three Bulls and Father Lacombe started the journey west. On the way, they visited with Lieutenant Governor Dewdney.

His travels convinced the chief that his had been right to encourage his people to adapt to new ways, for change was inevitable. He sometimes worked in the fields and in the winter time he moved into the house the government had built for him. When he recovered strength for another journey, he went to visit the Bloods in the southern plains who had not been faced with such an abrupt change and still managed to carry on their raiding and hunting activities. During Crowfoot's visit, the young warriors planned a raid on a hostile tribe though their chief, Red Crow, tried to restrain them. Crowfoot added his voice to the cause of peace, the elder wise men prevailed and a peace treaty was signed.

Though his health was failing, he managed another visit to the Assiniboines in Montana but there he was met with hostility on the part of the young braves who mocked his message of peace. When the situation became threatening, Crowfoot faced them courageously until their absent chief returned and rebuked them. Crowfoot was profoundly saddened by this encounter, not realising that after he left the Assiniboine camp, his influence and courage helped bring about a cessation of the raids on other tribes.

When he reached Blackfoot Crossing, exhausted after his travels, he took to his bed. During the spring of 1890, the medicine men went to his lodge and by their rituals tried to drive away the evil spirits. The agent sent a doctor to see him, but nothing could be done. He said farewell to his wives and friends and advised them to forget the past and face the new uncertain future. When news of his death spread, the whole camp mourned the loss of their great chief. The missionaries wanted to bury him as a Christian, but the Blackfeet, though accepting a coffin for the chief, insisted that it remain partially above ground as was the native custom. In the coffin were some of his possessions, including his knife and blanket and over the burial site they built a wooden shelter. Crowfoot's horse was shot so that its spirit could accompany that of its owner.

Messages of sympathy and tributes came from the Prime Minister, the Lieutenant Governor, missionaries, men of the North West Mounted Police and all those who had benefitted from the wisdom and heroism of the great man. With little control

over the events which in his lifetime devastated the ancient ways of the Blackfoot
nation, he had stood protectively over his
tribe with courage and foresight. Because he
chose peaceful solutions to the conflicts
which faced his people, The Blackfeet were
successful in surviving the great changes
which overtook them.

Chapter Seven

Maquinna

On March 29, 1778 a great throng of Nootka Indians lined the beach at Friendly Cove (now known as Resolution Cove) on the west coast of Vancouver Island. All eyes were fixed on the distant horizon where two tall ships loomed into view out of the overhanging clouds. Among the spectators, one commanding figure towered above the rest. That man was the Nootka chief known as Maquinna.

As far as we know, Maquinna was the son of a chief and he succeeded his father in 1778. For centuries, the Nootka lived in their coastal home undisturbed by European explorers. They were a sturdy race, of medium height, with broad faces and long muscular arms. Except for their heavy, dark eyebrows they looked very much like Chinese.

Because of the mild climate, the Nootka wore very little clothing. In the summer, the women wore a kind of apron made of woven cedar bark, and in winter they wore cloaks and dresses of the same material. When they were cold, the men wore woven cedar bark cloaks or robes made from sea otter fur. To keep out the rain, especially when they were out fishing in the Pacific Ocean, the men wore coats made of cedar bark stripes and straw hats shaped like flower pots. Both sexes sometimes wore beautiful blankets woven from dog or mountain goat hair, dyed yellow, black, and turquoise blue. Most of the time they went barefoot because moccasins were more trouble than they were worth in the damp climate.

What the Nootka lacked in clothing, they made up for in ornaments. In their ears and noses, they wore copper hoops, beads, abalone shells, and whales' teeth while bangles and bracelets adorned their necks and arms. For great events, such as feasts and war parties, and sometimes just for fun, they painted their faces white, black and red. Their black hair generally flowed down to their shoulders, but sometimes it was brushed straight upwards and held together with bracelets or feathers. Like most native people, the Nootka had scanty beards and the hairs that did appear were plucked out with tweezers.

For the most part, their food came from the sea, which teemed with salmon, cod, halibut, porpoises and whales. They also ate seaweed, as well as roots and berries. The land animals hunted were chiefly deer, bears and mountain goats. Farming was unknown to them, although they did grow some tobacco near the villages. Unlike other native people, the west coast indians did not smoke. Instead, they ground and dried the leaves and chewed the tobacco.

The Nootka were very clever fishermen and the only whale hunters in British Columbia. In April and May, they paddled far out to sea in their dug-out canoes to hunt the whale, sometimes many times larger than the canoe itself. The person who harpooned the huge mammal was usually a chief, such as Maquinna. After the catch, they towed the huge fish home to the village, where they were greeted with great ceremony.

The Nootka lived in large wooden houses with gabled roofs, elaborately decorated on the outside with carved and painted designs. Huge totem poles stood majestically at the entrance or at the ends of the houses. Like many of the west coast Indians, Maquinna's tribe had a summer and a winter village. The summer village was situated at Yuquot at the mouth of Nootka Sound and the winter village was at Tahsis.

A group of west coast indians with their canoe.
Reprinted, by permission,
Glenbow Archives: NH-1807-11

On that memorable day in March, the villagers disputed among themselves about the approaching ships. Some thought they were floating islands. Others believed that the ships carried one of the Nootka gods returning to live amongst them. Maquinna knew better. It seems that some of his people had already been in contact with Spanish explorers and Maquinna himself was the proud owner of two silver spoons that he had probably received from Spanish sailors.

He decided to investigate for himself.

Returning to his village he collected a large store of furs. Then he painted his face, donned a feather headdress and took his magic rattle, shaped like a large bird, in his hand. Accompanied by another chief and six braves, he launched a cedar canoe and paddled out to the first ship. The vessel was the *Discovery*, manned by Captain James Cook. Close behind it was the *Resolution* and its commander Captain George Bligh. On the voyage as well was the young George Vancouver.

As he neared the *Discovery*, Maquinna called out a friendly greeting in his own language. On deck, Captain Cook in his navy blue suit with gold braid and buttons, made signs of friendship and gestured to the chief to come aboard. Maquinna was wary at first. He might be taking his life in his hands if he boarded the white man's vessel. Finally his curiosity got the better of him and he climbed on board, followed by his seven companions.

Captain Cook received the men with great ceremony. Maquinna's stately bearing and great height marked him out as an important man and the captain was eager to impress him. The *Resolution* and the *Discovery* had been blown off course by heavy storms, the sailors were hungry and the vessels were badly in need of repairs. Cook knew that he had to have the native people on his side, so it was important to make friends with the chief. In return for

Maquinna's glossy furs, the captain presented the chief with several brightly colored blankets. Maquinna was so pleased with the exchange that he took off his fine sea otter coat and presented it to his host, who handed him his Captain's hat in return.

That night the crew came ashore and the friendly villagers welcomed them with a wolf dance. The newcomers stayed in the area almost a month while the carpenters repaired the mast of the Discovery and overhauled the canvas and rigging. Meanwhile, the men were feasted royally and provided with food and water for the return voyage. Maquinna made the most of the new opportunities. In return for salmon and furs, he received axes, knives, and all kinds of metal objects, all of which increased his wealth and prestige among the Nootka. But Captain Cook and his men probably had the best part of the bargain. When they left the island they had more than 300 furs, many of them sea otter, a very valuable fur in China.

After Cook's departure, other traders who heard about the valuable furs poured into the village. Maquinna controlled the trade with the newcomers. In time, he opened up passes to the inland sea and exchanged elk skins for sea otter. Soon his power and influence spread far into the interior and along the western sea board.

Sometimes the Europeans tried to trick the Nootka. Once, the captain of a small boat even poisoned some of Maquinna's men with rum laced with strychnine. In 1785, James Hanna, the captain of the *Sea Otter* arrived in Friendly Cove with a large cargo of knives, axes, pots, and bars of iron and copper. While Maquinna's men were trading with Hanna, one of them stole a chisel from the boat. The enraged captain opened fire on the natives, killing 20 people.

The following year a newcomer arrived in Friendly Cove with two ships. The man was Captain Strange who worked for the East India Company. Among the first men to greet the Captain was Maquinna. Strange was very impressed with the tall chief and found him very hospitable. Many of the sailors suffered from scurvy because of a lack of fresh vegetables. Seeing their distress, Maquinna collected green vegetation, boiled it and fed it to the men, and they recovered. During his stay, Strange admired the Nootka family life and the attachment that existed between Maquinna and his wife.

Before his departure, Strange decided to leave an agent in the village for a year. The man chosen was John Mackay, the surgeon's helper, who had cured Maquinna's son of a skin infection. Mackay was to study the native language and to treat minor illnesses, but he was warned not to attempt to treat anything serious. On his side, Maquinna promised to look after Mackay so well that the man would be as fat as a whale when Strange returned. From the ship's stores, Mackay was given a supply of clothes, blankets, dried beef, salt, rice, tea, sugar and tobacco, as well as garden seeds, grain and a male and female goat.

Maquinna also asked Strange to leave a musket and a pistol. Strange did not want the Chief to lay hands on a weapon, so he devised a clever plan. He told Maquinna that only a white man could handle a gun. In the hands of a native person, he said, the weapon would knock the man to the ground.

Maquinna was not convinced. Thereupon, Strange loaded the musket with a great deal of powder and handed it to the chief who took aim and fired. Of course the gun backfired and Maquinna keeled over as Strange had predicted! Complaining loudly about the pain in his arm, Maquinna vowed he would never touch the weapon again.

Mackay was the first white man to spend a whole year among the Nootka. He and Maquinna talked a good deal about their experiences and Maquinna gave him two slaves to help with the new garden. Mackay tried to teach the Nootka about the Christian religion, but without much success, for Maquinna was quite happy with the Nootka gods.

As time went on, the friendship between the two men began to wear thin. When Maquinna found out that Mackay was becoming too friendly with the native girls, he expelled the white man from the village and made him live in a hut. That winter happened to be harsher than usual and Mackay complained of hunger, although he was allowed six herrings a day like everyone else. To add insult to injury, the Nootka began to steal Mackay's supplies.

The following year when the sailing ship arrived to pick him up, Mackay was in disgrace. Unwashed, unshaven and in rags, he was such a sorry spectacle that one of the women on board ship fainted at the sight of him.

After Mackay's departure, Maquinna and his men were left in peace for a year. Then, another ship, commanded by Captain Meares, sailed into Friendly Cove. On board the ship was Maquinna's brother, Comekala. It seems Comekala had boarded a foreign boat some time earlier and before he knew what was happening, the boat was on its way to China. In China, he happened to meet Captain Meares who agreed to take him back to British Columbia. To curry favor with Maquinna, the shrewd captain treated Comekala like a prince and gave him many presents. When the boat docked at Friendly Cove, out stepped Comekala dressed in a scarlet cloak and a huge feathered hat, with copper ornaments dangling from his ears and carrying a large spit in his hand as a spear.

That night Maquinna held a feast and invited everyone to his lodge. The captain was pleased to see that Comekala did not seem to enjoy the whale blubber and other Nootka food as much as the other tribesmen. An "English" Comekala would be more likely to side with the white men and get them better bargains. To please Comekala still further, the captain persuaded Maquinna to arrange for a marriage between the returned wanderer and a royal princess. Unfortunately for Meares, Comekala soon went back to his Nootka ways. However, Meares did manage to get a piece of land from Maquinna. This land was to be the subject of dispute in years to come.

Hard on the heels of the British, an American ship under the command of Captain Robert Grey arrived in Friendly Cove to trade. The Americans offended Maquinna, so the Chief gathered his followers together and set out for his winter village at Tahsis. While he was gone, two Spanish ships sailed into the harbor under their commander Jose Martinez. The Spaniards claimed the navigation rights along the west coast and on the island itself.

When Maquinna returned to Yuquot, the village was in a turmoil. Martinez had confiscated the British ship and taken several prisoners. The large trees sheltering the houses had been cut down and new buildings crowded against the Nootka settlement. With the help of Chinese workers captured from the British, the Spaniards were constructing a fur factory at the head of Machalat Arm and some of the men were prospecting for gold.

Maquinna accepted the new situation as best he could and sold a piece of land in the village to Martinez. He attended a splendid ceremony at which Martinez and four priests dedicated the land to the Spanish crown. For the occasion, Maquinna was dressed in his finest robe, his hair festooned with the downy white feathers of baby eagles and carrying a long staff carved at the top like an eagle head. Beside him, also in ceremonial dress, was his brother Callicum.

After the ceremony, Callicum paddled out in his canoe to the Spanish ship to scold the Spaniards for capturing a British prisoner. On a boat nearby, Martinez saw one of his fellow countrymen making a friendly gesture to the Nootka chief. Fearing a treacherous attack, Martinez called out to Callicum, ordering him to come on board his own ship. Callicum refused. Taking his gun in his hand, Martinez fired at the chief and killed him.

That night, hot for revenge, Maquinna sent four men, their bodies blackened with charcoal, out to the Spanish boats to cut the anchors. As the vessels drifted out to sea, the Spaniards tried to kill the attackers but they were unable to see the pitch-black bodies in the darkness. Later, Callicum's remains were placed in a cedar box at the top of a tall tree as was the custom among the Nootka. Then Maquinna ordered every house in Yuquot to be burned to the ground and he led his men to Opitsat, the village of Callicum's father-in-law.

In the meantime, a Spaniard named Manuel Quimper was sent out to Friendly Cove. Later, two other Spanish officers, Don Francisco Eliza and Don Pedro Alberni, arrived on the scene. Knowing the great influence of Maquinna, the new arrivals did their best to win him over.

According to the story, Maquinna remained suspicious. Retreating into the woods, he refused to have anything to do with the newcomers. Alberni developed a clever strategem. Knowing that the Nootka had a great love of prestige, he had his men write a song in the Nootka language. At the edge of the woods the men sang the following song:

> Great is Maquinna
> Maquinna is a great chief
> Spain loves Maquinna

Maquinna called another chief to listen to the song, but by the time the man arrived the singing had stopped. Cautiously, Maquinna made his way out of the woods and called out to the Spaniards. "Sing it again," he said. When he appeared, the Spaniards heaped him with gifts and sang their song. Maquinna was completely won over.

All quarrels forgotten, the Spaniards and Nootka became the best of friends. Trading resumed and Alberni's men were free to work without fear of attack. As the weeks went by, the Spanish settlement began to take shape. The land was cleared, houses sprang up and a hospital was built for the sick. Maquinna even began to adopt some Spanish customs. On his visits to the settlement, he bowed low and doffed his hat in the manner of his hosts.

Back in England, the government viewed the Spanish settlement with alarm. They argued that they too had a right to settle on the island because of the land the Maquinna had sold to Captain Meares. Negotiators from each country were appointed to settle the dispute – Quardro for Spain and George Vancouver for England. Both men were reasonable people but they were unable to decide the case.

While the two men were on the island, Maquinna invited both of them to a great feast. On their arrival he escorted them into his lodge. Inside was a large platform to seat the honored guests, and around the room Maquinna's treasures were on view – furs, mirrors and ornaments of all kinds. After a feast served on silver platters, the entertainment began. Dressed as birds, animals, or fish, a parade of people performed a dance, each one imitating his own particular animal.

Soon after, the dispute between Spain and England was settled. The Spanish settlement was eventually destroyed and the British flag was hoisted in Friendly Cove. For a time no new settlers arrived. All that remained in Friendly Cove were a few ruins and overgrown gardens and the rats from the foreign ships. By 1795, Maquinna had brought his people back to Yuquot and rebuilt his village. Late that year a visitor reported that the old chief was very ill. Apparently, he died soon afterwards in his old home at Yuquot.

Glossary

Algonkians

A large number of tribes who lived in the eastern part of Canada from Ontario to the Atlantic Coast. They all spoke dialects of the same language (Algonkian) and lived almost entirely on hunting and fishing.

Algonkin

One of the largest tribes of the Algonkian family, after whom both the language and the whole group of tribes are named.

Bull Boat

A boat made by stretching skins over a wooden frame shaped like a circular basket. The boat was used by the prairie Indians.

Cache

A hiding place where food and other goods were hidden for safekeeping.

Calumet

A pipe used to burn tobacco as an offering to the Great Spirit and as a sign of friendship. The calumet was also a symbol of tribal power and unity. It had a long shaft painted in different colors and adorned with quills, heads, fur and feathers. The bowl was carved from stone or clay often engraved with designs.

Company of One Hundred Associates (Compagnie Des Cent Associes)

An organization of merchants and noblemen founded in 1627. A French law conferred the whole of the North American continent on the company and gave its members a monopoly on the fur trade. In return, the Associates promised to send 300 people to Canada each year, to support the settlers for three years and to provide each community with priests. The Company was dissolved in 1663.

Coureurs De Bois – Unlicensed Fur Traders of New France

Despite repeated warnings from the government, these renegades traded freely with the native people and played an important role in exploration and in establishing contact with the nature people

Donnée

A lay helper who sometimes accompanied priests on their missions.

Five Nations

See Iroquois.

Habitation – Settlement

The name is usually given to the group of houses constructed to shelter and protect the first settlers, e.g., the habitations at Post Royal and Quebec.

Hurons

A group of tribes which broke away from the Iroquoian community. A great trading nation, they acted as middlemen between the French and the northern tribes. Generally allied to the French, the Huron nation was destroyed by the Iroquois in 1650.

Illinois

the Illinios-Miami tribes lived in the Mississippi valley around the present state of Illinois.

Intendant

The most important administrative office in New France, eventually responsible for the administration of finance, justice and police in the colony.

Iroquois

(Also known as the Five Nations *and after they were joined by the Tuscanoras in 1722, the* Six Nations.

A league of five nations – the Mohawks, the Oneidas, the Onondagas, the Cayugas and the Senecas. They lived mainly in the present state of New York. The Hurons, the Tobacco Naiton, and the New Tribes, all of who lived in southern Ontario, were also Iroquoian tribes, but they did not belong to the league.

Pemmican

Dried meat, usually bison, beaten into coarse powder and mixed with melted fat and sometimes berries. The pemmican was cooled and packed in bison hide bags which could be carried long distances.

Peorias

One of the Illinois tribes.

Portage

A land route around an interruption in a waterway. When travellers were unable to continue on their journey by canoe, they hoisted their goods and canoes on their backs and continued until they reached the next section fo navigable water where they re-launched their boats.

Potlatch

A large celebration among the west coast Indian tribes, where wealth such as blankets, cedar boxes, fish, canoes and even slaves, were bestowed on others, or even ceremonially destroyed. On such occasions chiefs tried to outdo each other in generosity. Potlatches were held to honor new chiefs, to mourn the dead, and to mark other important occasions, and a great pottatch could last for days and even weeks.

Sachem

An Algonkian word meaning "chief".

Sagamite

A thin porridege made of husked corn mixed with fish, berried and/or whatever edibles were available.

Sagamo

See "Sachem."

Seigneurial System

Modeled after the French feudal system, it was started in the hop that the owner of a large grant of land would bring our settlers from France to cultivate the soil and make their homes in New France. The seigneur paid nothing for the land and settlers paid a small rent and worked six days each year for their masters.

Six Nations

See Iroquois.

Travois

A transportaion device among the Plains Indians. It was made of two long poles with a framwork at the back to hold baggage. The poles were lashed to the pike, a dog or a horse.

Voyageur

The name generally given to adventurous men who travelled by canoe into the interior of the country to trade with the native people.

Wampum

Originally made of white and purple sea shells and later of beads strung together into strings, belts and sashes. It was used by the Indians as money, oraments and ceremonial pledges. It was also used in the fur trade as a means of exchange. Wampum belts with particular patterns were used to cement treaties and on other important occasions. The designs in the wampum helped the native people to remember past events.

Selected Bibliography

Amherst, Jeffery *The Journals of Jeffery Amherst . . . from 1758 to 1763*. Edited by J. Clarence Webster. Toronto: Ryerson, 1931.

Chalmers, Harvey *Joseph Brant, Mohawk*. Toronto: Ryerson, 1955.

Charlevoix, Francis Xavier *History and General Description of New France*. Translated with notes by J. G. Shea. Chicago: Loyola University Press, 1744.

Colden, Cadwallader *The History of the Five Indian Naitons*. Ithaca, New York: Great Seal Books, 1727.

Cook, James *Voyages around the World*. Edited by John Burrow. London: Adam and Charles Black, 1784.

Costain, Thomas B. *The White and the Gold*. New York: Doubleday, 1954.

Crompton, F. C. B. *Lahontan* Toronto: Nelson, 1925. Excerpts from the journals of Baron Lahonton, first published in 1703.

Dempsey, Hugh A. *Crowfoot*. Edmonton: Hurtig, 1972.

_____*Dictionary of Canadian Biography*. Toronto: University of Toronto Press, 1966-.

Eccles, W.J. *Frontiac, the Coutier Governor*. Toronto : McCelland and Stewart, 1959.

Grinde, Donald A. *The Iroquois and the Founding of the American Nation*. San Francisco: Indian Historical Press, 1977.

Hacker, Carlotta. *Crowfoot*. Don Mills, Ontario: Fitzhenry Whiteside, 1977.

Hale, Horatio. *The Iroquois Book of Rites*. Philadelphia: Brinton, 1883.

Jeness, Diamond. *The Indians of Canada*. Ottawa: National Museum of Canada, 1977.

Jones, Elizabeth. *Gentlemen and Jesuits*. Toronto: University of Toronto Press, 1986.

Kinietz, W.V. *The Indians of the Great Lakes*. Ann Arbor, Michigan: University Press, 1940.

Lescarbot, Marc. *History*. 3 vols. Reprinted and translated by I. Grant. Toronto: Champlain Society, 1609.

Leechman, John Douglas. *Nature Tribes of Canada*. Toronto: Gage, 1965.

Marie D'Incarnation. *The Selected Letters of Marie d'Incarnation*. Selected, edited and translated by Joyce Marshall. Toronto: Oxford University Press, 1639-72.

Marquis, Thomas Guthrie. *The War Chief of the Ottawas*. Toronto: University of Toronto Press, 1964.

Monture, Ethel Brant. *Famous Indians*. Toronto: Clarke, Irwin, 1960.

Parkman, Francis, *The Conspiracy of Pontiac*. 2 vols. Boston: Little Brown, 1889.

Peckham, Howard H. *Pontiac and the Indian Uprising*. Princeton, New Jersey: Princeton University Press, 1947.

Stone, W.L. *Life of Joseph Brant – Thayendanegeu*. 2 vols. New York: Blake, 1838.

Thwartes, R.G., ed. and trans. *The Jesuit Relations and Allied Documents (1610-1791)*. New York: Pageant Books, 1959.

Vancouver, George. *A voyage of Discovery to the North Pacific Ocean*. Edited by John Vancouver. London: Adan and Charles Black, 1798.